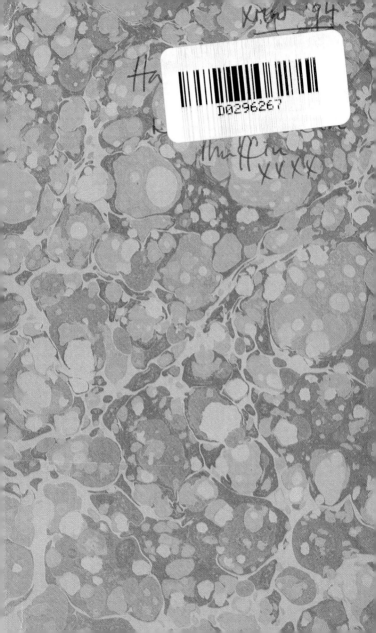

THE ROMANTIC POETS

THE ROMANTIC POETS

Byron · Keats · Shelley Wordsworth

Selected and with introductions by
Geoffrey Moore and Peter Porter

AURUM PRESS

CONTENTS

PERCY BYSSHE SHELLEY

WILLIAM WORDSWORTH

Lord Byron

INTRODUCTION

With Shakespeare, George Gordon, Lord Byron is the most celebrated English poet outside the English-speaking world, and one of the supreme literary figures within it. He established single-handed the special aura of Romanticism which excited whole generations of European poets, including such remarkable men as Gérard de Nerval, Pushkin and Lermontov. His narrative poems, *The Corsair* and *Parisina*, and his speculative plays, *Marino Faliero* and *The Two Foscari*, were turned into nineteenth-century Italian operas by Donizetti and Verdi, and even Goethe, already an old man, when Byron was writing, felt the force of his influence.

Byron's death from fever at Missolonighi in 1824, at the head of an army he had raised and paid for himself, led directly to the liberation of Greece. Fired by his martyrdom, the British public forced a reluctant government to send a fleet against the Turks at the Battle of Navarino and so pave the way for Greek independence.

Byron's life was characteristically short in the manner of Romantic poets – he died at thirty-six, his contemporaries Shelley and Keats at twenty-nine and twenty-six respectively. But at his death he was the most famous poet in Europe and the most notorious sexual adventurer. While an undergraduate at Cambridge he kept a pet bear in the porter's lodge; on the Grand Tour he posed for his portrait in Albanian costume and swam the Hellespont, lived with brigands and visited seraglios. His liaisons with aristocratic beauties such as Lady Caroline Lamb and Lady Oxford kept his name before a fascinated public, and the scandal of his disputed divorce from an heiress,

Annabella Milbanke, whom he nicknamed 'the Princess of Parallelograms' for her reserved and scientific composure, destroyed his standing in English society. He left England for good in 1816 and wrote his greatest poetry in exile.

Yet the truly remarkable thing about Byron is his poetry – on the one hand, it is revolutionary in its romantic self-dramatization; on the other, it places him as the true inheritor of the Augustan precision and control of Alexander Pope. He wrote with wonderful fluency and his copious output ranges widely over many subjects and scenes, from picturesque travelogues of the Levant to house-parties in the depths of the English countryside. Byron was the worldliest of poets, yet he kept a freshness of utterance in everything he wrote. He was melancholy and ebullient at once, generous and bitter, a poet of the realm and a convinced democrat, his only consistency being his moral and physical courage.

Nowadays we see Byron as very different from his contemporaries' view of him as the supreme Romantic. Working from his best poems, *The Vision of Judgment*, *Beppo* and *Don Juan*, we esteem him as a pioneer of the conviction that 'light' or social verse may be as fully perceptive of the human condition as the solemn contemplation of Nature and Man practised by Wordsworth and his followers. But this revision must not be taken too far. Byron wrote a formidable body of poetry charged with that aura of doubt and exaggerated despair which is the hallmark of Romanticism. The fashionable image he created for himself made him the cynosure of Europe and gave us our adjective 'Byronic'. It is represented best today in *Childe Harold's Pilgrimage*. The publication of the first canto of this poem in 1812 made Byron famous overnight.

Childe Harold is constructed by the simplest and most effective means. Harold's European and Levantine travels form the background to the poem; Harold himself is just a peg for Byron to hang his observations on. The set-piece descriptions, however, are magnificent, as the stanzas devoted to Venice show.

The irony of Byron's long period of exile – 1816 to 1824, most of which he passed in Italy, at Venice, Ravenna, Pisa and Genoa – is the way in which it made him brood on his homeland, resulting in a magnificent set of letters back to friends in London and turning him increasingly to scenes from his English triumphs in the poems he wrote from 1818 onwards. These letters, which have been published in unexpurgated form only in the past decade, are perhaps the richest in all English literature. They paint the sharpest and most wide-ranging picture of the way people lived, netting the whole panorama realistically in words at once precise and evocative. The same realism leavened by humour became his chosen style in poetry. He borrowed the stanza known as *ottava rima* from Italian poetry and produced, in *Don Juan*, the most readable long poem in our language. At the end, Byron was writing verse as accurate, moving and witty as the prose he had always used in his letters.

It is a peculiarity of Byron's poetry that his finest work is to be found in his long poems. Extended passages from *Childe Harold* and *Don Juan* lie at the heart of this achievement, and I have, in consequence, chosen liberally from these for this brief selection of Byron's work. To help place each extract I have printed it under an explanatory heading of my own devising. Its source is given in a note on p.52.

PETER PORTER

Martial, Book 1, Epigram 1

He unto whom thou art so partial,
Oh, reader! is the well-known Martial,
The Epigrammatist: while living,
Give him the fame thou wouldst be giving;
So shall he hear, and feel, and know it –
    Post-obits rarely reach a poet.

Adrian's Address to His Soul
When Dying

'Animula, vagula, blandula'

Ah! gentle, fleeting, wavering sprite,
Friend and associate of this clay!
    To what unknown region borne,
Wilt thou now wing thy distant flight?
No more with wonted humour gay,
    But pallid, cheerless, and forlorn.

From
CHILDE HAROLD'S PILGRIMAGE

Harold in Greece

And yet how lovely in thine age of woe,
Land of lost gods and godlike men! art thou!
Thy vales of ever-green, thy hills of snow
Proclaim thee Nature's varied favourite now:
Thy fanes, thy temples to thy surface bow,
Commingling slowly with heroic earth,
Broke by the share of every rustic plough:
So perish monuments of mortal birth,
So perish all in turn, save well-recorded Worth;

Save where some solitary column mourns
Above its prostrate brethren of the cave;
Save where Tritonia's airy shrine adorns
Colonna's cliff, and gleams along the wave;
Save o'er some warrior's half-forgotten grave,
Where the grey stones and unmolested grass
Ages, but not oblivion, feebly brave,
While strangers only not regardless pass,
Lingering like me, perchance, to gaze, and sigh 'Alas!'

Yet are thy skies as blue, thy crags as wild;
Sweet are thy groves, and verdant are thy fields,
Thine olive ripe as when Minerva smil'd,
And still his honied wealth Hymettus yields;
There the blithe bee his fragrant fortress builds,
The freeborn wanderer of thy mountain-air,
Apollo still thy long, long summer gilds,
Still in his beam Mendeli's marbles glare;
Art, Glory, Freedom fail, but Nature still is fair.

Where'er we tread 'tis haunted, holy ground;
No earth of thine is lost in vulgar mould,
But one vast realm of wonder spreads around,
All the Muse's tales seem truly old,
Till the sense aches with gazing to behold
The scenes our earliest dreams have dwelt upon:
Each hill and dale, each deepening glen and
    wold
Defies the power which crush'd thy temples
    gone:
Age shakes Athena's tower, but spares gray
    Marathon.

Harold's Lyric by the Rhine

The castled crag of Drachenfels
Frowns o'er the wide and winding Rhine,
Whose breast of waters broadly swells
Between the banks which bear the vine,
And hills all rich with blossomed trees,
And fields which promise corn and wine,
And scattered cities crowning these,
Whose far white walls along them shine,
Have strewed a scene, which I should see
With double joy wert *thou* with me!

And peasant girls, with deep blue eyes,
And hands which offer early flowers,
Walk smiling o'er this paradise;
Above, the frequent feudal towers
Through green leaves lift their walls of grey,
And many a rock which steeply lours,
And noble arch in proud decay,
Look o'er this vale of vintage-bowers;
But one thing want these banks of Rhine, –
Thy gentle hand to clasp in mine!

I send the lilies given to me;
Though long before thy hand they touch,
I know that they must withered be,
But yet reject them not as such;
For I have cherish'd them as dear,
Because they yet may meet thine eye,
And guide thy soul to mine even here,
When thou behold'st them droopng nigh,
And knowst them gathered by the Rhine,
And offered from my heart to thine!

The river nobly foams and flows,
The charm of this enchanted ground,
And all its thousand turns disclose
Some fresher beauty varying round;
The haughtiest breast its wish might bound
Through life to dwell delighted here;
Nor could on earth a spot be found
To nature and to me so dear,
Could thy dear eyes in following mine
Still sweeten more these banks of Rhine!

Harold Alone

I have not loved the world, nor the world me;
I have not flattered its rank breath, nor bow'd
To its idolatries a patient knee, –
Nor coin'd my cheek to smiles, – nor cried aloud
In worship of an echo; in the crowd
They could not deem me one of such; I stood
Among them, but not of them; in a shroud
Of thoughts which were not their thoughts, and
    still could,
Had I not filed my mind, which thus itself subdued.

I have not loved the world, nor the world me, –
But let us part fair foes; I do believe,
Though I have found them not, that there may
    be
Words which are things, – hopes which will not
    deceive,
And virtues which are merciful, nor weave
Snares for the failing: I would also deem
O'er others' griefs that some sincerely grieve;
That two, or one, are almost what they seem, –
That goodness is no name, and happiness no
    dream.

Harold in Venice

I stood in Venice, on the Bridge of Sighs;
A palace and a prison on each hand:
I saw from out the wave her structures rise
As from the stroke of the enchanter's wand:
A thousand years their cloudy wings expand
Around me, and a dying Glory smiles
O'er the far times, when many a subject land
Look'd to the winged Lion's marble piles,
Where Venice sate in state, thron'd on her
    hundred isles!

She looks a sea Cybele, fresh from ocean,
Rising with her tiara of proud towers
At airy distance, with majestic motion,
A ruler of the waters and their powers:
And such she was; – her daughters had their
    dowers
From spoils of nations, and the exhaustless East
Pour'd in her lap all gems in sparkling showers.
In purple was she robed, and of her feast
Monarchs partook, and deem'd their dignity
    increas'd.

In Venice Tasso's echoes are no more,
And silent rows the songless gondolier;
Her palaces are crumbling to the shore,
And music meets not always now the ear:
Those days are gone – but Beauty still is here.
States fall, arts fade – but Nature doth not die,
Nor yet forget how Venice once was dear,
The pleasant place of all festivity,
The revel of the earth, the masque of Italy!

But unto us she hath a spell beyond
Her name in story, and her long array
Of mighty shadows, whose dim forms despond
Above the dogeless city's vanish'd sway;
Ours is a trophy which will not decay
With the Rialto; Shylock and the Moor,
And Pierre, can not be swept or worn away –
The keystones of the arch! though all were o'er,
For us repeopled were the solitary shore.

Before St Mark still glow his steeds of brass,
Their gilded collars glittering in the sun;
But is not Doria's menace come to pass?
Are they *not bridled*? – Venice, lost and won,
Her thirteen hundred years of freedom done,
Sinks, like a sea-weed, into whence she rose!
Better be whelm'd beneath the waves, and shun,
Even in destruction's depth, her foreign foes,
From whom submission wrings an infamous repose.

Statues of glass – all shiver'd – the long file
Of her dead Doges are declin'd to dust;
But where they dwelt, the vast and sumptuous
    pile
Bespeaks the pageant of their splendid trust;
Their sceptre broken, and their sword in rust,
Have yielded to the stranger: empty halls,
Thin streets, and foreign aspects, such as must
Too oft remind her who and what enthrals,
Have flung a desolate cloud o'er Venice' lovely
    walls.

Harold's Philosophy

From mighty wrongs to petty perfidy
Have I not seen what human things could do?
From the loud roar of foaming calumny
To the small whisper of the as paltry few,
And subtler venom of the reptile crew,
The Janus glance of whose significant eye,
Learning to lie with silence, would *seem* true,
And without utterance, save the shrug or sigh,
Deal round to happy fools its speechless obloquy.

But I have lived, and have not lived in vain:
My mind may lose its force, my blood its fire,
And my frame perish even in conquering pain;
But there is that within me which shall tire
Torture and Time, and breathe when I expire;
Something unearthly, which they deem not of,
Like the remembered tone of a mute lyre,
Shall on their softened spirits sink, and move
In hearts all rocky now the late remorse of love.

The seal is set. – Now welcome, thou dread power!
Nameless, yet thus omnipotent, which here
Walk'st in the shadow of the midnight hour
With a deep awe, yet all distinct from fear;
Thy haunts are ever where the dead walls rear
Their ivy mantles, and the solemn scene
Derives from thee a sense so deep and clear
That we become a part of what has been,
And grow unto the spot, all-seeing but unseen.

She Walks in Beauty

She walks in beauty, like the night
   Of cloudless climes and starry skies;
And all that's best of dark and bright
   Meet in her aspect and her eyes:
Thus mellow'd to that tender light
   Which heaven to gaudy day denies.

One shade the more, one ray the less,
   Had half impair'd the nameless grace
Which waves in every raven tress,
   Or softly lightens o'er her face;
Where thoughts serenely sweet express
   How pure, how dear their dwelling place.

And on that cheek, and o'er that brow,
   So soft, so calm, yet eloquent,
The smiles that win, the tints that glow,
   But tell of days in goodness spent,
A mind at peace with all below,
   A heart whose love is innocent!

So, We'll Go No More A Roving

So, we'll go no more a roving
   So late into the night,
Though the heart be still as loving,
   And the moon be still as bright.

For the sword outwears its sheath,
   And the soul wears out the breast,
And the heart must pause to breathe,
   And love itself have rest.

Though the night was made for loving,
   And the day returns too soon,
Yet we'll go no more a roving
   By the light of the moon.

From THE ISLAND

Here, in this grotto of the wave-worn shore,
They passed the tropic's red meridian o'er;
Nor long the hours – they never paused o'er time,
Unbroken by the clock's funereal chime,
Which deals the daily pittance of our span,
And points and mocks with iron laugh at man.
What deemed they of the future or the past?
The present, like a tyrant, held them fast:
Their hour-glass was the sea-sand, and the tide,
Like her smooth billow, saw their moments glide;
Their clock the sun, in his unbounded tower;
They reckoned not, whose day was but an hour;
The nightingale, their only vesper-bell,
Sung sweetly to the rose the day's farewell;
The broad sun set, but not with lingering sweep,
As in the north he mellows o'er the deep;
But fiery, full, and fierce, as if he left
The world for ever, earth of light bereft,
Plunged with red forehead down along the wave,
As dives a hero headlong to his grave.
Then rose they, looking first along the skies,
And then for light into each other's eyes,
Wondering that summer showed so brief a sun,
And asking if indeed the day were done.

When We Two Parted

When we two parted
    In silence and tears
Half broken-hearted
    To sever for years,
Pale grew thy cheek and cold,
    Colder thy kiss;
Truly that hour foretold
    Sorrow to this.

The dew of the morning
    Sunk chill on my brow –
It felt like the warning
    Of what I feel now.
Thy vows are all broken,
    And light is thy fame;
I hear thy name spoken,
    And share in its shame.

They name thee before me,
　　A knell to mine ear;
A shudder comes o'er me –
　　Why wert thou so dear?
They know not I knew thee,
　　Who knew thee too well: –
Long, long shall I rue thee,
　　Too deeply to tell.

In secret we met –
　　In silence I grieve,
That thy heart could forget,
　　Thy spirit deceive.
If I should meet thee
　　After long years,
How should I greet thee! –
　　With silence and tears.

From THE VISION OF JUDGMENT

On Robert Southey

He said – (I only give the heads) – he said,
  He meant no harm in scribbling; 'twas his way
Upon all topics; 'twas, besides, his bread,
  Of which he butter'd both sides; 'twould delay
Too long the assembly (he was pleased to dread)
  And take up rather more time than a day,
To name his works – he would but cite a few –
Wat Tyler – Rhymes on Blenheim – Waterloo.

He had written praises of a regicide;
  He had written praises of all kings whatever,
He had written for republics far and wide,
  And then against them bitterer than ever,
For pantisocracy he once had cried
  Aloud, a scheme less moral than 'twas clever;
Then grew a hearty antijacobin –
Had turn'd his coat – and would have turn'd his skin.

He had sung against all battles, and again
  In their high praise and glory: he had call'd
Reviewing 'the ungentle craft,' and then
  Become as base a critic as ere crawl'd –
Fed, paid, and pamper'd by the very men
  By whom his muse and morals had been maul'd:
He had written much blank verse, and blanker prose,
And more of both than any body knows.

From BEPPO

On Italy and England

With all its sinful doings, I must say,
   That Italy's a pleasant place to me,
Who love to see the Sun shine every day,
   And vines (not nail'd to walls) from tree to tree
Festoon'd, much like the back scene of a play,
   Or melodrame, which people flock to see,
When the first act is ended by a dance
In vineyards copied from the south of France.

I love the language, that soft bastard Latin,
   Which melts like kisses from a female mouth,
And sounds as if it should be writ on satin,
   With syllables which breathe of the sweet South,
And gentle liquids gliding all so pat in,
   That not a single accent seems uncouth,
Like our harsh northern whistling, grunting guttural,
Which we're oblig'd to hiss, and spit, and sputter all.

I like the women too (forgive my folly),
   From the rich peasant-cheek of ruddy bronze,
And large black eyes that flash on you a volley
   Of rays that say a thousand things at once,
To the high dama's brow, more melancholy,
   But clear, and with a wild and liquid glance,
Heart on her lips, and soul within her eyes,
Soft as her clime, and sunny as her skies.

'England! with all thy faults I love thee still,'
    I said at Calais, and have not forgot it;
I like to speak and lucubrate my fill;
    I like the government (but that is not it);
I like the freedom of the press and quill;
    I like the Habeas Corpus (when we've got it);
I like a parliamentary debate,
Particularly when 'tis not too late;

I like the taxes, when they're not too many;
    I like a sea-coal fire, when not too dear;
I like a beef-steak, too, as well as any;
    Have no objection to a pot of beer;
I like the weather, when it is not rainy,
    That is, I like two months of every year,
And so God save the Regent, Church, and King!
Which means that I like all and everything.

Our standing army, and disbanded seamen,
    Poor's rate, Reform, my own, the nation's debt,
Our little riots just to show we are free men,
    Our trifling bankruptcies in the Gazette,
Our cloudy climate and our chilly women,
    All these I can forgive, and those forget,
And greatly venerate our recent glories,
And wish they were not owing to the Tories.

From DON JUAN

Fragment on the back of the Ms. of Canto 1

I would to heaven that I were so much clay,
    As I am blood, bone, marrow, passion, feeling –
Because at least the past were passed away
    And for the future – (but I write this reeling,
Having got drunk exceedingly today,
    So that I seem to stand upon the ceiling)
I say – the future is a serious matter –
And so – for God's sake – hock and soda-water!

Comparative Morality

'Tis a sad thing, I cannot choose but say,
　　And all the fault of that indecent sun,
Who cannot leave alone our helpless clay,
　　But will keep baking, broiling, burning on,
That howsoever people fast and pray
　　The flesh is frail, and so the soul undone:
What men call gallantry, and gods adultery,
Is much more common where the climate's sultry.

Happy the nations of the moral north!
　　Where all is virtue, and the winter season
Sends sin, without a rag on, shivering forth;
　　('Twas snow that brought St Anthony to
　　　　reason);
Where juries cast up what a wife is worth
　　By laying whate'er sum, in mulct, they please on
The lover, who must pay a handsome price,
Because it is a marketable vice.

First Love

'Tis sweet to win, no matter how, one's laurels
    By blood or ink; 'tis sweet to put an end
To strife; 'tis sometimes sweet to have our quarrels,
    Particularly with a tiresome friend;
Sweet is old wine in bottles, ale in barrels;
    Dear is the helpless creature we defend
Against the world; and dear the schoolboy spot
We ne'er forget, though there we are forgot.

But sweeter still than this, than these, than all,
    Is first and passionate love – it stands alone,
Like Adam's recollection of his fall;
    The tree of knowledge has been pluck'd –
        all's known –
And life yields nothing further to recall
    Worthy of this ambrosial sin, so shown,
No doubt in fable, as the unforgiven
Fire which Prometheus filch'd for us from heaven.

Poetical Commandments

If ever I should condescend to prose,
    I'll write poetical commandments, which
Shall supersede beyond all doubt all those
    That went before; in these I shall enrich
My text with many things that no one knows,
    And carry precept to the highest pitch:
I'll call the work 'Longinus o'er a Bottle,
Or, Every Poet his *own* Aristotle'.

Thou shalt believe in Milton, Dryden, Pope;
    Thou shalt not set up Wordsworth, Coleridge,
      Southey;
Because the first is crazed beyond all hope,
    The second drunk, the third so quaint and
      mouthey:
With Crabbe it may be difficult to cope,
    And Campbell's Hippocrene is somewhat
      drouthy:
Thou shalt not steal from Samuel Rogers, nor
Commit – flirtation with the muse of Moore.

Haidée's Island and a Hangover

It was a wild and breaker-beaten coast,
    With cliffs above, and a broad sandy shore,
Guarded by shoals and rocks as by an host,
    With here and there a creek, whose aspect wore
A better welcome to the tempest-tost;
    And rarely ceased the haughty billow's roar,
Save on the dead long summer days, which make
The outstretch'd ocean glitter like a lake.

And the small ripple spilt upon the beach
    Scarcely o'erpass'd the cream of your
        champaigne,
When o'er the brim the sparkling bumpers reach,
    That spring-dew of the spirit! the heart's rain!
Few things surpass old wine; and they may preach
    Who please, – the more because they preach in
        vain, –
Let us have wine and woman, mirth and laughter,
Sermons and soda water the day after.

Juan and Haidée in Love

They look'd up to the sky, whose floating glow
   Spread like a rosy ocean, vast and bright;
They gazed upon the glittering sea below,
   Whence the broad moon rose circling into sight;
They heard the wave's splash, and the wind so low,
   And saw each other's dark eyes darting light
Into each other – and, beholding this,
Their lips drew near, and clung into a kiss;

A long, long kiss, a kiss of youth, and love,
   And beauty, all concentrating like rays
Into one focus, kindled from above;
   Such kisses as belong to early days,
Where heart, and soul, and sense, in concert
     move,
   And the blood's lava, and the pulse a blaze,
Each kiss a heart-quake, – for a kiss's strength,
I think, it must be reckon'd by its length.

They were alone, but not alone as they
   Who shut in chambers think it loneliness;
The silent ocean, and the starlight bay,
   The twilight glow, which momently grew less,
The voiceless sands, and dropping caves, that lay
   Around them, made them to each other press,
As if there were no life beneath the sky
Save theirs, and that their life could never die.

They feared no eyes nor ears on that lone beach,
    They felt no terrors from the night; they were
All in all to each other; though their speech
    Was broken words, they *thought* a language
        there, –
And all the burning tongues the passions teach
    Found in one sigh the best interpreter
Of nature's oracle – first love, – that all
Which Eve has left her daughters since her fall.

Alas! they were so young, so beautiful,
    So lonely, loving, helpless, and the hour
Was that in which the heart is always full
    And, having o'er itself no further power,
Prompts deeds eternity can not annul,
    But pays off moments in an endless shower
Of hell-fire – all prepared for people giving
Pleasure or pain to one another living.

They look upon each other, and their eyes
    Gleam in the moonlight; and her white arm
        clasps
Round Juan's head, and his around her lies
    Half buried in the tresses which it grasps;
She sits upon his knee, and drinks his sighs,
    He hers, until they end in broken gasps;
And thus they form a group that's quite antique,
Half naked, loving, natural, and Greek.

Haidée's Death

Thus lived – thus died she; never more on her
    Shall sorrow light, or shame. She was not made
Through years or moons the inner weight to bear,
    Which colder hearts endure till they are laid
By age in earth; her days and pleasure were
    Brief, but delightful – such as had not staid
Long with her destiny; but she sleeps well
By the sea shore, whereon she loved to dwell.

That isle is now all desolate and bare,
    Its dwellings down, its tenants past away;
None but her own and father's grave is there,
    And nothing outward tells of human clay;
Ye could not know where lies a thing so fair,
    No stone is there to show, no tongue to say
What was; no dirge, except the hollow sea's,
Mourns o'er the beauty of the Cyclades.

The Taking of Ismail and the Horrors of War

The town was taken – whether he might yield
    Himself or bastion, little mattered now;
His stubborn valour was no future shield.
    Ismail's no more! The crescent's silver bow
Sunk, and the crimson cross glared o'er the field,
    But red with no *redeeming* gore: the glow
Of burning streets, like moonlight on the water,
Was imaged back in blood, the sea of slaughter.

All that the mind would shrink from of excesses;
    All that the body perpetrates of bad;
All that we read, hear, dream, of man's distresses;
    All that the Devil would do if run stark mad;
All that defies the worst which pen expresses;
    All by which Hell is peopled, or as sad
As Hell – mere mortals who their power abuse, –
Was here (as heretofore and since) let loose.

If here and there some transient trait of pity
    Was shown, and some more noble heart broke
        through
Its bloody bond, and saved perhaps some pretty
    Child, or an aged, helpless man or two –
What's this in one annihilated city,
    Where thousand loves, and ties, and duties
        grew?
Cockneys of London! Muscadins of Paris!
Just ponder what a pious pastime war is.

The Duke of Wellington

Oh, Wellington! (or 'Vilainton' – for Fame
  Sounds the heroic syllables both ways;
France could not even conquer your great name,
  But punned it down to this facetious phrase –
Beating or beaten she will laugh the same) –
  You have obtained great pensions and much
      praise;
Glory like yours should any dare gainsay,
Humanity would rise, and thunder 'Nay!'

I don't think that you used Kinnaird quite well
  In Marinêt's affair – in fact 'twas shabby,
And like some other things won't do to tell
  Upon your tomb in Westminster's old abbey.
Upon the rest 'tis not worth while to dwell,
  Such tales being for the tea hours of some tabby;
But though your years as *man* tend fast to zero,
In fact your Grace is still but a *young Hero*.

Though Britain owes (and pays you too) so much,
  Yet Europe doubtless owes you greatly more:
You have repaired Legitimacy's crutch, –
  A prop not quite so certain as before:
The Spanish, and the French, as well as Dutch,
  Have seen, and felt, how strongly you *restore*;
And Waterloo has made the world your debtor –
(I wish your bards would sing it rather better).

You are 'the best of cut-throats:' – do not start;
    The phrase is Shakespeare's, and not misapplied: –
War's a brain-spattering, windpipe-slitting art,
    Unless her cause by Right be sanctified.
If you have acted *once* a generous part,
    The World, not the World's masters, will
        decide,
And I shall be delighted to learn who,
Save you and yours, have gained by Waterloo?

I am no flatterer – you've supped full of flattery:
    They say you like it too – 'tis no great wonder:
He whose whole life has been assault and battery,
    At last may get a little tired of thunder;
And swallowing eulogy much more than satire, he
    May like being praised for every lucky blunder,
Called 'Saviour of the Nations' – not yet saved,
And Europe's Liberator – still enslaved.

I've done. Now go and dine from off the plate
    Presented by the Prince of the Brazils,
And send the sentinel before your gate
    A slice or two from your luxurious meals:
He fought, but has not fed so well of late.
    Some hunger too they say the people feels: –
There is no doubt that you deserve your ration,
But pray give back a little to the nation.

The Prospect of London

A mighty mass of brick, and smoke, and shipping,
  Dirty and dusky, but as wide as eye
Could reach, with here and there a sail just
      skipping
  In sight, then lost amidst the forestry
Of masts; a wilderness of steeples peeping
  On tiptoe, through their sea-coal canopy;
A huge, dun cupola, like a foolscap crown
On a fool's head – and there is London Town!

But Juan saw not this: each wreath of smoke
  Appeared to him but as the magic vapour
Of some alchymic furnace, from whence broke
  The wealth of worlds (a wealth of tax and
      paper):
The gloomy clouds, which o'er it as a yoke
  Are bowed, and put the sun out like a taper,
Were nothing but the natural atmosphere,
Extremely wholesome, though but rarely clear.

Juan on Shooter's Hill

Don Juan had got out on Shooter's Hill;
  Sunset the time, the place the same declivity
Which looks along that vale of good and ill
  Where London streets ferment in full activity;
While every thing around was calm and still,
  Except the creak of wheels, which on their pivot he
Heard, – and that bee-like, bubbling, busy hum
Of cities, that boil over with their scum: –

I say, Don Juan, wrapt in contemplation,
  Walked on behind his carriage, o'er the summit,
And lost in wonder of so great a nation,
  Gave way to't, since he could not overcome it.
'And here,' he cried, 'is Freedom's chosen station;
  Here peals the people's voice, nor can entomb it
Racks, prisons, inquisitions; resurrection
Awaits it, each new meeting or election.

'Here are chaste wives, pure lives; here people pay
  But what they please; and if that things be dear,
'Tis only that they love to throw away
  Their cash, to show how much they have a year.
Here laws are all inviolate; none lay
  Traps for the traveller, every highway's clear:
Here' – he was interrupted by a knife,
With, 'Damn your eyes! your money or your life!'

These freeborn sounds proceeded from four pads,
    In ambush laid, who had perceived him loiter
Behind his carriage; and, like handy lads,
    Had seized the lucky hour to reconnoitre,
In which the heedless gentleman who gads
    Upon the road, unless he prove a fighter,
May find himself within that isle of riches
Exposed to lose his life as well as breeches.

Juan, who did not understand a word
    Of English, save their shibboleth, 'God damn!'
And even that he had so rarely heard,
    He sometimes thought 'twas only their 'Salām,'
Or 'God be with you!' – and 'tis not absurd
    To think so; for half English as I am
(To my misfortune) never can I say
I heard them wish 'God with you,' save that way; –

Juan yet quickly understood their gesture,
    And being somewhat choleric and sudden,
Drew forth a pocket-pistol from his vesture,
    And fired it into one assailant's pudding –
Who fell as rolls an ox o'er in his pasture,
    And roared out, as he writhed his native mud in,
Unto his nearest follower or henchman,
'Oh Jack! I'm floored by that 'ere bloody
        Frenchman!'

Newstead Abbey Recalled

The mansion's self was vast and venerable,
   With more of the monastic than has been
Elsewhere preserved: the cloisters still were stable,
   The cells too and refectory, I ween:
An exquisite small chapel had been able,
   Still unimpair'd, to decorate the scene;
The rest had been reform'd, replaced, or sunk,
And spoke more of the baron than the monk.

Huge halls, long galleries, spacious chambers, join'd
   By no quite lawful marriage of the Arts,
Might shock a Connoisseur; but when combined,
   Form'd a whole which, irregular in parts,
Yet left a grand impression on the mind,
   At least of those whose eyes are in their hearts.
We gaze upon a Giant for his stature,
Nor judge at first if all be true to Nature.

Steel Barons, molten the next generation
   To silken rows of gay and garter'd Earls,
Glanced from the walls in goodly preservation;
   And Lady Marys blooming into girls,
With fair long locks, had also kept their station:
   And Countesses mature in robes and pearls:
Also some beauties of Sir Peter Lely,
Whose drapery hints we may admire them freely.

Judges in very formidable ermine
    Were there, with brows that did not much invite
The accused to think their Lordships would
        determine
    His cause by leaning much from might to right:
Bishops, who had not left a single sermon;
    Attornies-General, awful to the sight,
As hinting more (unless our judgments warp us)
Of the 'Star Chamber' than of 'Habeas Corpus.'

Generals, some all in armour, of the old
    And iron time, ere Lead had ta'en the lead;
Others in wigs of Marlborough's martial fold,
    Huger than twelve of our degenerate breed:
Lordlings with staves of white, or keys of gold:
    Nimrods, whose canvas scarce contain'd the
        steed;
And here and there some stern high Patriot stood,
Who could not get the place for which he sued.

On This Day I Complete My Thirty-Sixth Year

'Tis time this heart should be unmoved,
   Since others it hath ceased to move:
Yet though I cannot be beloved,
          Still let me love!

My days are in the yellow leaf;
   The flowers and fruits of Love are gone;
The worm – the canker, and the grief
          Are mine alone!

The fire that on my bosom preys
   Is lone as some Volcanic Isle;
No torch is kindled at its blaze
          A funeral pile!

The hope, the fear, the jealous care,
   The exalted portion of the pain
And power of Love I cannot share,
          But wear the chain.

But 'tis not *thus* – and 'tis not *here*
   Such thoughts should shake my Soul, nor *now*
Where Glory decks the hero's bier
          Or binds his brow.

The Sword, the Banner, and the Field,
    Glory and Greece around us see!
The Spartan borne upon his shield
                Was not more free!

Awake (not Greece – she *is* awake!)
    Awake, my Spirit! think through *whom*
Thy life-blood tracks its parent lake
                And then strike home!

Tread those reviving passions down
    Unworthy Manhood – unto thee
Indifferent should the smile or frown
                Of Beauty be.

If thou regret'st thy Youth, *why live?*
    The land of honourable Death
Is here: – up to the Field, and give
                Away thy Breath!

Seek out – less often sought than found –
    A Soldier's Grave, for thee the best;
Then look around, and choose thy Ground,
                And take thy Rest!

SOURCES OF THE EXTRACTS

'Harold in Greece': *Childe Harold's Pilgrimage*, Canto 2, stanzas 85 to 88.

'Harold's Lyric by the Rhine': *Childe Harold*, Canto 3.

'Harold Alone': *Childe Harold*, Canto 3, stanzas 113 to 114.

'Harold in Venice': *Childe Harold*, Canto 4, stanzas 1 to 4, 13, 15.

'Harold's Philosophy': *Childe Harold*, Canto 4, stanzas 136 to 138.

'Here in this grotto . . . ': *The Island*, Canto 2, section 15.

'On King George the Third': *The Vision of Judgment*, stanzas 7 to 10.

'On Robert Southey': *The Vision of Judgment*, stanzas 96 to 98.

'On Italy and England': *Beppo*, stanzas 41, 44 to 45, 47 to 49.

'Comparative Morality': *Don Juan*, Canto 1, stanzas 63 to 64.

'First Love': *Don Juan*, Canto 1, stanzas 126 to 127.

'Poetical Commandments': *Don Juan*, Canto 1, stanzas 204 to 205.

'Haidée's Island and a Hangover': *Don Juan*, Canto 2, stanzas 177 to 178.

'Juan and Haidée in Love': *Don Juan*, Canto 2, stanzas 185 to 186, 188 to 189, 192, 194.

'Haidée's Death': *Don Juan*, Canto 4, stanzas 71 to 72.

'The Taking of Ismail and the Horrors of War': *Don Juan*, Canto 8, stanzas 122 to 124.

'The Duke of Wellington': *Don Juan*, Canto 9, stanzas 1 to 6.

'The Prospect of London': *Don Juan*, Canto 10, stanzas 82 to 83.

'Juan on Shooter's Hill': *Don Juan*, Canto 11, stanzas 8 to 13.

'Newstead Abbey Recalled': *Don Juan*, Canto 13, stanzas 66 to 70.

NOTES ON THE PICTURES

John Keats

INTRODUCTION

John Keats was born on 31 October 1795 and died on 23 February 1821, eight months before his twenty-sixth birthday. In that short space of time he produced work of greater quality than many other notable poets have achieved in double his life-span.

From the first, his life was dogged by tragedy and illness. His father, the manager of a livery stable, was killed in a riding accident when Keats was eight; his mother died of tuberculosis when he was fourteen. From the family home in Moorfields, Keats was sent to Clarke's school in Enfield and at the age of fifteen was apprenticed by his grandmother to an apothecary-surgeon. The eldest of five children, he had a particularly close relationship with his brother George, to whom some of his best letters were written.

Keats's letters are the wonder of the age. They are of as much interest as the poems themselves, and it is quite remarkable that a very young man could have produced such wisdom and insight. His famous doctrine of Negative Capability, put forward in a letter to George and Tom when he was twenty-two years old, defines it as the state in which a poet is 'capable of being in uncertainties, mysteries, doubts, without any irritable reaching after fact and reason'. This is the cast of mind which he said Shakespeare possessed 'so enormously' – and which, we might add, he also possessed when he wrote the great Odes.

These poems, which have added so much to English literature, were written when he was dying of tuberculosis and nursing his brother, who had the same disease. Keats's life is, in fact, a paradox. As a tuberculosis sufferer, he should have been a will-o'-the-wisp, but he was in fact sturdy and pugnacious, despite his height of only five feet one inch. Like his protagonist in the 'Ode on Melancholy', he 'burst Joy's grape against his palate fine'. Of all the great Romantic poets he is the most sensuous, without ever lapsing into the sensual, for his nature was at the same time pure and fine.

Before he developed his idolatry of Shakespeare, Keats was much drawn to Spenser. From all the evidence, his sure-footed 'Imitation of Spenser' was probably written early in 1814, when he was just nineteen. In 1815 he enrolled as a medical student at Guy's Hospital, becoming licensed to practise as an apothecary in 1816.

Keats's first major work, *Endymion*, was begun on 18 April 1817, at Carisbrooke on the Isle of Wight. On 8 October in that year he wrote to his friend Benjamin Bailey that he was going to make it 'a trial of my Powers of Imagination . . . by which I must take 4000 Lines of one bare circumstance and fill them with Poetry'. At this stage he still favoured the heroic couplet, which he forsook the next year for the Miltonic blank verse of *Hyperion*.

His brother Tom died in December 1818, while Keats was working on *Hyperion*. In the meantime he had fallen hopelessly in love with Fanny Brawne, who may have inspired 'The Eve of St Agnes'.

In April 1819 Keats wrote 'La Belle Dame sans Merci' and 'Ode to Psyche' and, later in the same year, the 'Ode on a Grecian Urn', 'Ode on Melancholy', 'Ode to a Nightingale' and 'To Autumn'. By that time his medical training told him that there was little which could save him from terminal illness.

On 3 February 1820 he noted that he was coughing arterial blood, the first unmistakable sign of the disease that was to kill him. He sailed to Italy in September, hoping that a milder climate might effect at least some temporary improvement, but alas it did not, and he lingered only a few more months.

In his lifetime Keats had to suffer brutal and unwarranted criticism. He was labelled by Lockhart in *Blackwood's* a member of the 'Cockney School' and both *Endymion* and *Hyperion* were savagely attacked. Although deeply wounded, Keats wrote to George, 'I think I shall be among the English Poets after my death.'

And so he is. Poets as divergent as Tennyson, Arnold and Hopkins all attested to the influence of Keats's poetry on them. He does not, like Shelley, soar into the empyrean but gives us something which is in the end more satisfying. His poetry is a continual celebration of life. When he saw a sparrow pecking about on the gravel, he did not merely identify himself with the bird, he became it.

When we read Keats's poems, we become him. We empathize not merely with his sentiments but with the whole man, for in his power to subdue his own ego, Keats raises us above the petty and the trivial. 'The roaring of the wind is my wife,' he wrote to George and Georgiana Keats in October 1818, 'and the Stars through the window pane are my Children.' How much more apt and fitting an epitaph this is than his own self-deprecating 'Here lies one whose name was writ in water.'

GEOFFREY MOORE

I

In drear-nighted December,
    Too happy, happy tree,
Thy Branches ne'er remember
    Their green felicity:
The north cannot undo them,
With a sleety whistle through them;
Nor frozen thawings glue them
    From budding at the prime.

II

In drear-nighted December,
    Too happy, happy Brook,
Thy bubblings ne'er remember
    Apollo's summer look;
But with a sweet forgetting,
They stay their crystal fretting,
Never, never petting
    About the frozen time.

III

Ah! would 'twere so with many
    A gentle girl and boy!
But were there ever any
    Writh'd not of passed joy?
The feel of not to feel it,
When there is none to heal it,
Nor numbed sense to steel it,
    Was never said in rhyme.

Happy is England! I could be content
  To see no other verdure than its own;
  To feel no other breezes than are blown
Through its tall woods with high romances blent:
Yet do I sometimes feel a languishment
  For skies Italian, and an inward groan
  To sit upon an Alp as on a throne,
And half forget what world or worldling meant.
Happy is England, sweet her artless daughters;
  Enough their simple loveliness for me,
    Enough their whitest arms in silence clinging:
  Yet do I often warmly burn to see
    Beauties of deeper glance, and hear their
        singing,
And float with them about the summer waters.

On First Looking into Chapman's Homer

Much have I travell'd in the realms of gold,
　　And many goodly states and kingdoms seen;
　　Round many western islands have I been
Which bards in fealty to Apollo hold.
Oft of one wide expanse had I been told
　　That deep-brow'd Homer ruled as his demesne;
　　Yet did I never breathe its pure serene
Till I heard Chapman speak out loud and bold:
Then felt I like some watcher of the skies
　　When a new planet swims into his ken;
Or like stout Cortez when with eagle eyes
　　He star'd at the Pacific – and all his men
Look'd at each other with a wild surmise –
　　Silent, upon a peak in Darien.

On the Grasshopper and Cricket

The poetry of earth is never dead:
    When all the birds are faint with the hot sun,
    And hide in cooling trees, a voice will run
From hedge to hedge about the new-mown mead;
That is the Grasshopper's – he takes the lead
    In summer luxury, – he has never done
    With his delights; for when tired out with fun
He rests at ease beneath some pleasant weed.
The poetry of earth is ceasing never:
    On a lone winter evening, when the frost
        Has wrought a silence, from the stove there
        shrills
The Cricket's song, in warmth increasing ever,
    And seems to one in drowsiness half lost,
        The Grasshopper's among some grassy hills.

On the Sea

It keeps eternal whisperings around
   Desolate shores, and with its mighty swell
   Gluts twice ten thousand Caverns, till the spell
Of Hecate leaves them their old shadowy sound.
Often 'tis in such gentle temper found,
   That scarcely will the very smallest shell
   Be mov'd for days from where it sometime fell,
When last the winds of Heaven were unbound.
Oh ye! who have your eye-balls vex'd and tir'd,
   Feast them upon the wideness of the Sea;
     Oh ye! whose ears are dinn'd with uproar rude,
   Or fed too much with cloying melody –
     Sit ye near some old Cavern's Mouth and
      brood,
Until ye start, as if the sea-nymphs quir'd!

From ENDYMION:
A Poetic Romance

Book 1

A thing of beauty is a joy for ever:
Its loveliness increases; it will never
Pass into nothingness; but still will keep
A bower quiet for us, and a sleep
Full of sweet dreams, and health, and quiet
　　breathing.
Therefore, on every morrow, are we wreathing
A flowery band to bind us to the earth,
Spite of despondence, of the inhuman dearth
Of noble natures, of the gloomy days,
Of all the unhealthy and o'er-darkened ways
Made for our searching: yes, in spite of all,
Some shape of beauty moves away the pall
From our dark spirits. Such the sun, the moon,
Trees old, and young, sprouting a shady boon
For simple sheep; and such are daffodils
With the green world they live in; and clear rills
That for themselves a cooling covert make
'Gainst the hot season; the mid forest brake,
Rich with a sprinkling of fair musk-rose blooms:
And such too is the grandeur of the dooms
We have imagined for the mighty dead;
All lovely tales that we have heard or read:
An endless fountain of immortal drink,
Pouring unto us from the heaven's brink.

Nor do we merely feel these essences
For one short hour; no, even as the trees
That whisper round a temple become soon
Dear as the temple's self, so does the moon,
The passion poesy, glories infinite,
Haunt us till they become a cheering light
Unto our souls, and bound to us so fast,
That, whether there be shine, or gloom o'ercast,
They alway must be with us, or we die.

Therefore, 'tis with full happiness that I
Will trace the story of Endymion.
The very music of the name has gone
Into my being, and each pleasant scene
Is growing fresh before me as the green
Of our own vallies: so I will begin
Now while I cannot hear the city's din;
Now while the early budders are just new,
And run in mazes of the youngest hue
About old forests; while the willow trails
Its delicate amber; and the dairy pails
Bring home increase of milk. And, as the year
Grows lush in juicy stalks, I'll smoothly steer
My little boat, for many quiet hours,
With streams that deepen freshly into bowers.
Many and many a verse I hope to write,
Before the daisies, vermeil rimm'd and white,
Hide in deep herbage; and ere yet the bees
Hum about globes of clover and sweet peas,
I must be near the middle of my story.

O may no wintry season, bare and hoary,
See it half finish'd: but let Autumn bold,
With universal tinge of sober gold,
Be all about me when I make an end.
And now at once, adventuresome, I send
My herald thought into a wilderness:
There let its trumpet blow, and quickly dress
My uncertain path with green, that I may speed
Easily onward, thorough flowers and weed.

   Upon the sides of Latmos was outspread
A mighty forest; for the moist earth fed
So plenteously all weed-hidden roots
Into o'er-hanging boughs, and precious fruits.
And it had gloomy shades, sequestered deep,
Where no man went; and if from shepherd's keep
A lamb stray'd far a-down those inmost glens,
Never again saw he the happy pens
Whither his brethren, bleating with content,
Over the hills at every nightfall went.
Among the shepherds, 'twas believed ever,
That not one fleecy lamb which thus did sever
From the white flock, but pass'd unworried
By angry wolf, or pard with prying head,
Until it came to some unfooted plains
Where fed the herds of Pan; aye great his gains
Who thus one lamb did lose. Paths there were
     many,

Winding through palmy fern, and rushes fenny,
And ivy banks; all leading pleasantly
To a wide lawn, whence one could only see
Stems thronging all around between the swell
Of turf and slanting branches: who could tell
The freshness of the space of heaven above,
Edg'd round with dark tree tops? through which a
    dove
Would often beat its wings, and often too
A little cloud would move across the blue.

When I have fears that I may cease to be
　　Before my pen has glean'd my teeming brain,
Before high-piled books, in charactery,
　　Hold like rich garners the full ripen'd grain;
When I behold, upon the night's starr'd face,
　　Huge cloudy symbols of a high romance,
And think that I may never live to trace
　　Their shadows, with the magic hand of chance;
And when I feel, fair creature of an hour,
　　That I shall never look upon thee more,
Never have relish in the faery power
　　Of unreflecting love; – then on the shore
Of the wide world I stand alone, and think
Till love and fame to nothingness do sink.

From HYPERION:
A Fragment

Book 1

Deep in the shady sadness of a vale
Far sunken from the healthy breath of morn,
Far from the fiery noon, and eve's one star,
Sat gray-hair'd Saturn, quiet as a stone,
Still as the silence round about his lair;
Forest on forest hung about his head
Like cloud on cloud. No stir of air was there,
Not so much life as on a summer's day
Robs not one light seed from the feather'd grass,
But where the dead leaf fell, there did it rest.
A stream went voiceless by, still deadened more
By reason of his fallen divinity
Spreading a shade: the Naiad 'mid her reeds
Press'd her cold finger closer to her lips.

Along the margin-sand large foot-marks went,
No further than to where his feet had stray'd,
And slept there since. Upon the sodden ground
His old right hand lay nerveless, listless, dead,
Unsceptred; and his realmless eyes were closed;
While his bow'd head seem'd list'ning to the
    Earth,
His ancient mother, for some comfort yet.

It seem'd no force could wake him from his
place;
But there came one, who with a kindred hand
Touch'd his wide shoulders, after bending low
With reverence, though to one who knew it not.
She was a Goddess of the infant world;
By her in stature the tall Amazon
Had stood a pigmy's height: she would have ta'en
Achilles by the hair and bent his neck;
Or with a finger stay'd Ixion's wheel.
Her face was large as that of Memphian sphinx,
Pedestal'd haply in a palace court,
When sages look'd to Egypt for their lore.
But oh! how unlike marble was that face:

How beautiful, if sorrow had not made
Sorrow more beautiful than Beauty's self.
There was a listening fear in her regard,
As if calamity had but begun;
As if the vanward clouds of evil days
Had spent their malice, and the sullen rear
Was with its stored thunder labouring up.
One hand she press'd upon that aching spot
Where beats the human heart, as if just there,
Though an immortal, she felt cruel pain;
The other upon Saturn's bended neck
She laid, and to the level of his ear

Leaning with parted lips, some words she spake
In solemn tenour and deep organ tone;
Some mourning words, which in our feeble tongue
Would come in these like accents; O how frail
To that large utterance of the early Gods!
'Saturn, look up! – though wherefore, poor old
        King?
'I have no comfort for thee, no not one:
'I cannot say, "O wherefore sleepest thou?"
'For heaven is parted from thee, and the earth
'Knows thee not, thus afflicted, for a God;
'And ocean too, with all its solemn noise,
'Has from thy sceptre pass'd; and all the air
'Is emptied of thine hoary majesty.
'Thy thunder, conscious of the new command,
'Rumbles reluctant o'er our fallen house;
'And thy sharp lightning in unpractis'd hands
'Scorches and burns our once serene domain.
'O aching time! O moments big as years!
'All as ye pass swell out the monstrous truth,
'And press it so upon our weary griefs
'That unbelief has not a space to breathe.
'Saturn, sleep on: – O thoughtless, why did I
'Thus violate thy slumbrous solitude?
'Why should I ope thy melancholy eyes?
'Saturn, sleep on! while at thy feet I weep.'

As when, upon a tranced summer-night,
Those green-rob'd senators of mighty woods,
Tall oaks, branch-charmed by the earnest stars,
Dream, and so dream all night without a stir,
Save from one gradual solitary gust
Which comes upon the silence, and dies off,
As if the ebbing air had but one wave;
So came these words and went; the while in tears
She touch'd her fair large forehead to the ground,
Just where her falling hair might be outspread
A soft and silken mat for Saturn's feet.

Fancy

Ever let the fancy roam,
Pleasure never is at home;
At a touch sweet Pleasure melteth,
Like to bubbles when rain pelteth;
Then let winged Fancy wander
Through the thought still spread beyond her;
Open wide the mind's cage-door,
She'll dart forth, and cloudward soar,
O sweet Fancy! let her loose;
Summer's joys are spoilt by use,
And the enjoying of the Spring
Fades as does its blossoming;
Autumn's red-lipp'd fruitage too,
Blushing through the mist and dew,
Cloys with tasting: What do then?
Sit thee by the ingle, when
The sear faggot blazes bright,
Spirit of a winter's night;
When the soundless earth is muffled,
And the caked snow is shuffled
From the ploughboy's heavy shoon;
When the Night doth meet the Noon
In a dark conspiracy
To banish Even from her sky.
Sit thee there, and send abroad,
With a mind self-overaw'd,
Fancy, high-commission'd: – send her!

She has vassals to attend her:
She will bring, in spite of frost,
Beauties that the earth hath lost;
She will bring thee, all together,
All delights of summer weather;
All the buds and bells of May,
From dewy sward or thorny spray;
All the heaped Autumn's wealth,
With a still, mysterious stealth;
She will mix these pleasures up
Like three fit wines in a cup,
And thou shalt quaff it: – thou shalt hear
Distant harvest-carols clear;
Rustle of the reaped corn;
Sweet birds antheming the morn:
And, in the same moment – hark!
'Tis the early April lark,
Or the rooks, with busy caw,
Foraging for sticks and straw.
Thou shalt, at one glance, behold
The daisy and the marigold;
White-plum'd lillies, and the first
Hedge-grown primrose that hath burst;
Shaded hyacinth, alway
Sapphire queen of the mid-May;
And every leaf, and every flower
Pearled with the self-same shower.
Thou shalt see the field-mouse peep

Meagre from its celled sleep;
And the snake all winter-thin
Cast on sunny bank its skin;
Freckled nest-eggs thou shalt see
Hatching in the hawthorn-tree,
When the hen-bird's wing doth rest
Quiet on her mossy nest;
Then the hurry and alarm
When the bee-hive casts its swarm;
Acorns ripe down-pattering,
While the autumn breezes sing.

Oh, sweet Fancy! let her loose;
Every thing is spoilt by use:
Where's the cheek that doth not fade,
Too much gaz'd at? Where's the maid
Whose lip mature is ever new?
Where's the eye, however blue,
Doth not weary? Where's the face
One would meet in every place?
Where's the voice, however soft,
One would hear so very oft?
At a touch sweet Pleasure melteth
Like to bubbles when rain pelteth.
Let, then, winged Fancy find
Thee a mistress to thy mind:
Dulcet-eyed as Ceres' daughter,
Ere the God of Torment taught her

How to frown and how to chide;
With a waist and with a side
White as Hebe's, when her zone
Slipt its golden clasp, and down
Fell her kirtle to her feet,
While she held the goblet sweet,
And Jove grew languid. – Break the mesh
Of the Fancy's silken leash;
Quickly break her prison-string
And such joys as these she'll bring –
Let the winged Fancy roam,
Pleasure never is at home.

La Belle Dame sans Merci

I

O, what can ail thee, knight-at-arms,
   Alone and palely loitering?
The sedge has wither'd from the lake,
   And no birds sing.

II

O, what can ail thee, knight-at-arms,
   So haggard and so woe-begone?
The squirrel's granary is full,
   And the harvest's done.

III

I see a lilly on thy brow,
   With anguish moist and fever dew;
And on thy cheeks a fading rose
   Fast withereth too.

IV

I met a lady in the meads,
   Full beautiful – a faery's child,
Her hair was long, her foot was light,
   And her eyes were wild.

V

I made a garland for her head,
    And bracelets too, and fragrant zone;
She look'd at me as she did love,
    And made sweet moan.

VI

I set her on my pacing steed,
    And nothing else saw all day long;
For sidelong would she bend, and sing
    A faery's song.

VII

She found me roots of relish sweet,
    And honey wild, and manna dew,
And sure in language strange she said –
    'I love thee true'.

VIII

She took me to her elfin grot,
    And there she wept and sigh'd full sore,
And there I shut her wild wild eyes
    With kisses four.

IX

And there she lulled me asleep
　　And there I dream'd – Ah! woe betide!
The latest dream I ever dream'd
　　On the cold hill side.

X

I saw pale kings and princes too,
　　Pale warriors, death-pale were they all;
They cried – 'La Belle Dame sans Merci
　　Hath thee in thrall!'

XI

I saw their starved lips in the gloam,
　　With horrid warning gaped wide,
And I awoke and found me here,
　　On the cold hill's side

XII

And this is why I sojourn here
　　Alone and palely loitering,
Though the sedge has wither'd from the lake,
　　And no birds sing.

Ode to Psyche

O Goddess! hear these tuneless numbers, wrung
　　By sweet enforcement and remembrance dear,
And pardon that thy secrets should be sung
　　Even into thine own soft-conched ear:
Surely I dreamt to-day, or did I see
　　The winged Psyche with awaken'd eyes?
I wander'd in a forest thoughtlessly,
　　And, on the sudden, fainting with surprise,
Saw two fair creatures, couched side by side
　　In deepest grass, beneath the whisp'ring roof
　　Of leaves and trembled blossoms, where there
　　　　ran
　　　　　　A brooklet, scarce espied:

'Mid hush'd, cool-rooted flowers, fragrant-eyed,
　　Blue, silver-white, and budded Tyrian,
They lay calm-breathing on the bedded grass;
　　Their arms embraced, and their pinions too;
　　Their lips touch'd not, but had not bade adieu,
As if disjoined by soft-handed slumber,
And ready still past kisses to outnumber
　　At tender eye-dawn of aurorean love:
　　　　The winged boy I knew;
　　But who wast thou, O happy, happy dove?
　　　　　　His Psyche true!

O latest born and loveliest vision far
    Of all Olympus' faded hierarchy!
Fairer than Phoebe's sapphire-region'd star,
    Or Vesper, amorous glow-worm of the sky;
Fairer than these, though temple thou hast none,
            Nor altar heap'd with flowers;
Nor virgin-choir to make delicious moan
            Upon the midnight hours;
No voice, no lute, no pipe, no incense sweet
    From chain-swung censer teeming;
No shrine, no grove, no oracle, no heat
    Of pale-mouth'd prophet dreaming.

O brightest! though too late for antique vows,
    Too, too late for the fond believing lyre,
When holy were the haunted forest boughs,
    Holy the air, the water, and the fire;
Yet even in these days so far retir'd
    From happy pieties, thy lucent fans,
    Fluttering among the faint Olympians,
I see, and sing, by my own eyes inspir'd.
So let me be thy choir, and make a moan
            Upon the midnight hours;
Thy voice, thy lute, thy pipe, thy incense sweet
    From swinged censer teeming;
Thy shrine, thy grove, thy oracle, thy heat
    Of pale-mouth'd prophet dreaming.

Yes, I will be thy priest, and build a fane
  In some untrodden region of my mind,
Where branched thoughts, new grown with
      pleasant pain,
  Instead of pines shall murmur in the wind:
Far, far around shall those dark-cluster'd trees
  Fledge the wild-ridged mountains steep by
      steep;
And there by zephyrs, streams, and birds, and
      bees,
  The moss-lain Dryads shall be lull'd to sleep;
And in the midst of this wide quietness
A rosy sanctuary will I dress
With the wreath'd trellis of a working brain,
  With buds, and bells, and stars without a name,
With all the gardener Fancy e'er could feign,
  Who breeding flowers, will never breed the
      same;
And there shall be for thee all soft delight
  That shadowy thought can win,
A bright torch, and a casement ope at night,
  To let the warm Love in!

Ode to a Nightingale

I

My heart aches, and a drowsy numbness pains
   My sense, as though of hemlock I had drunk,
Or emptied some dull opiate to the drains
   One minute past, and Lethe-wards had sunk:
'Tis not through envy of thy happy lot,
   But being too happy in thine happiness, –
      That thou, light-winged Dryad of the trees,
         In some melodious plot
   Of beechen green, and shadows numberless,
      Singest of summer in full-throated ease.

II

O, for a draught of vintage! that hath been
   Cool'd a long age in the deep-delved earth,
Tasting of Flora and the country green,
   Dance, and Provençal song, and sunburnt
      mirth!
O for a beaker full of the warm South,
   Full of the true, the blushful Hippocrene,
      With beaded bubbles winking at the brim,
         And purple-stained mouth;
   That I might drink, and leave the world
      unseen,
      And with thee fade away into the forest dim:

III

Fade far away, dissolve, and quite forget
    What thou among the leaves hast never known,
The weariness, the fever, and the fret
    Here, where men sit and hear each other groan;
Where palsy shakes a few, sad, last gray hairs,
    Where youth grows pale, and spectre-thin, and
          dies;
        Where but to think is to be full of sorrow
            And leaden-eyed despairs,
        Where Beauty cannot keep her lustrous eyes,
        Or new Love pine at them beyond
           to-morrow.

IV

Away! away! for I will fly to thee,
    Not charioted by Bacchus and his pards,
But on the viewless wings of Poesy,
    Though the dull brain perplexes and retards:
Already with thee! tender is the night,
    And haply the Queen-Moon is on her throne,
        Cluster'd around by all her starry Fays;
          But here there is no light,
    Save what from heaven is with the breezes
        blown
        Through verdurous glooms and winding
          mossy ways.

V

I cannot see what flowers are at my feet,
    Nor what soft incense hangs upon the boughs,
But, in embalmed darkness, guess each sweet
    Wherewith the seasonable month endows
The grass, the thicket, and the fruit-tree wild;
    White hawthorn, and the pastoral eglantine;
        Fast fading violets cover'd up in leaves;
            And mid-May's eldest child,
    The coming musk-rose, full of dewy wine,
        The murmurous haunt of flies on summer
            eves.

VI

Darkling I listen; and, for many a time
    I have been half in love with easeful Death,
Call'd him soft names in many a mused rhyme,
    To take into the air my quiet breath;
Now more than ever seems it rich to die,
    To cease upon the midnight with no pain,
        While though art pouring forth thy soul
            abroad
            In such an ecstasy!
    Still wouldst thou sing, and I have ears in
        vain —
            To thy high requiem become a sod.

VII

Thou wast not born for death, immortal Bird!
  No hungry generations tread thee down;
The voice I hear this passing night was heard
  In ancient days by emperor and clown:
Perhaps the self-same song that found a path
    Through the sad heart of Ruth, when, sick for
        home,
      She stood in tears amid the alien corn;
        The same that oft-times hath
    Charm'd magic casements, opening on the foam
    Of perilous seas, in faery lands forlorn.

VIII

Forlorn! the very word is like a bell
  To toll me back from thee to my sole self!
Adieu! the fancy cannot cheat so well
  As she is fam'd to do, deceiving elf.
Adieu! adieu! thy plaintive anthem fades
    Past the near meadows, over the still stream,
      Up the hill-side; and now 'tis buried deep
        In the next valley-glades:
    Was it a vision, or a waking dream?
      Fled is that music: – Do I wake or sleep?

Ode on a Grecian Urn

I

Thou still unravish'd bride of quietness,
　Thou foster-child of silence and slow time,
Sylvan historian, who canst thus express
　A flowery tale more sweetly than our rhyme:
What leaf-fring'd legend haunts about thy shape
　Of deities or mortals, or of both,
　　In Tempe or the dales of Arcady?
　What men or gods are these? What maidens
　　loth?
What mad pursuit? What struggle to escape?
　　What pipes and timbrels? What wild ecstasy?

II

Heard melodies are sweet, but those unheard
　Are sweeter; therefore, ye soft pipes, play on;
Not to the sensual ear, but, more endear'd,
　Pipe to the spirit ditties of no tone:
Fair youth, beneath the trees, thou canst not
　　leave
　Thy song, nor ever can those trees be bare;
　　Bold Lover, never, never canst thou kiss,

Though winning near the goal – yet, do not
    grieve;
  She cannot fade, though thou hast not thy
      bliss,
    For ever wilt thou love, and she be fair!

III

Ah, happy, happy boughs! that cannot shed
  Your leaves, nor ever bid the Spring adieu;
And, happy melodist, unwearied,
  For ever piping songs for ever new;
More happy love! more happy, happy love!
  For ever warm and still to be enjoy'd,
    For ever panting, and for ever young;
All breathing human passion far above,
  That leaves a heart high-sorrowful and cloy'd,
    A burning forehead, and a parching tongue.

IV

Who are these coming to the sacrifice?
  To what green altar, O mysterious priest,
Lead'st thou that heifer lowing at the skies,
  And all her silken flanks with garlands drest?
What little town by river or sea shore,
  Or mountain-built with peaceful citadel,
    Is emptied of this folk, this pious morn?

And, little town, thy streets for evermore
   Will silent be; and not a soul to tell
      Why thou art desolate, can e'er return.

V

O Attic shape! Fair attitude! with brede
   Of marble men and maidens overwrought,
With forest branches and the trodden weed;
   Thou, silent form, dost tease us out of thought
As doth eternity: Cold Pastoral!
   When old age shall this generation waste,
     Thou shalt remain, in midst of other woe
Than ours, a friend to man, to whom thou say'st,
   'Beauty is truth, truth beauty,' – that is all
     Ye know on earth, and all ye need to know.

Bright star, would I were stedfast as thou art –
    Not in lone splendour hung aloft the night
And watching, with eternal lids apart,
    Like nature's patient, sleepless Eremite,
The moving waters at their priestlike task
    Of pure ablution round earth's human shores,
Or grazing on the new soft-fallen mask
    Of snow upon the mountains and the moors –
No – yet still stedfast, still unchangeable,
    Pillow'd upon my fair love's ripening breast,
To feel for ever its soft fall and swell,
    Awake for ever in a sweet unrest,
Still, still to hear her tender-taken breath,
And so live ever – or else swoon to death.

Ode on Melancholy

I

No, no, go not to Lethe, neither twist
    Wolf's-bane, tight-rooted, for its poisonous
        wine;
Nor suffer thy pale forehead to be kiss'd
    By nightshade, ruby grape of Proserpine;
Make not your rosary of yew-berries,
    Nor let the beetle, nor the death-moth be
      Your mournful Psyche, nor the downy owl
A partner in your sorrow's mysteries;
    For shade to shade will come too drowsily,
      And drown the wakeful anguish of the soul.

II

But when the melancholy fit shall fall
    Sudden from heaven like a weeping cloud,
That fosters the droop-headed flowers all,
    And hides the green hill in an April shroud;
Then glut thy sorrow on a morning rose,
    Or on the rainbow of the salt sand-wave,
      Or on the wealth of globed peonies;
Or if thy mistress some rich anger shows,
    Emprison her soft hand, and let her rave,
      And feed deep, deep upon her peerless eyes.

III

She dwells with Beauty – Beauty that must die;
    And Joy, whose hand is ever at his lips
Bidding adieu; and aching Pleasure nigh,
    Turning to Poison while the bee-mouth sips:
Ay, in the very temple of delight
    Veil'd Melancholy has her sovran shrine,
      Though seen of none save him whose
        strenuous tongue
    Can burst Joy's grape against his palate fine;
His soul shall taste the sadness of her might,
      And be among her cloudy trophies hung.

To Autumn

I

Season of mists and mellow fruitfulness,
   Close bosom-friend of the maturing sun;
Conspiring with him how to load and bless
   With fruit the vines that round the thatch-eves
       run;
To bend with apples the moss'd cottage-trees,
   And fill all fruit with ripeness to the core;
     To swell the gourd, and plump the hazel
       shells
   With a sweet kernel; to set budding more,
And still more, later flowers for the bees,
Until they think warm days will never cease,
     For Summer has o'er-brimm'd their clammy
       cells.

II

Who hath not seen thee oft amid thy store?
   Sometimes whoever seeks abroad may find
Thee sitting careless on a granary floor,
   Thy hair soft-lifted by the winnowing wind;
Or on a half-reap'd furrow sound asleep,

Drows'd with the fume of poppies, while thy
     hook
   Spares the next swath and all its twined
      flowers:
And sometimes like a gleaner thou dost keep
   Steady thy laden head across a brook;
   Or by a cyder-press, with patient look,
      Thou watchest the last oozings hours by
         hours.

III

Where are the songs of Spring? Ay, where are
     they?
   Think not of them, thou hast thy music too, –
While barred clouds bloom the soft-dying day,
   And touch the stubble-plains with rosy hue;
Then in a wailful choir the small gnats mourn
   Among the river sallows, borne aloft
      Or sinking as the light wind lives or dies;
And full-grown lambs loud bleat from hilly bourn;
   Hedge-crickets sing; and now the treble soft
   The red-breast whistles from a garden-croft;
      And gathering swallows twitter in the skies.

This living hand, now warm and capable
Of earnest grasping, would, if it were cold
And in the icy silence of the tomb,
So haunt thy days and chill thy dreaming nights
That thou wouldst wish thine own heart dry of
        blood
So in my veins red life might stream again,
And thou be conscience-calm'd – see here it is –
I hold it towards you.

NOTES ON THE PICTURES

Percy Bysshe Shelley

INTRODUCTION

It is a paradox that Shelley and Byron, the most popular of the English Romantic poets, hardly deserve the description at all. Each lived a tempestuous life, and was a spectacularly visible embodiment of Romanticism, but each wrote in an older and more industrious tradition. You must look to Wordsworth, Coleridge and Keats for the real achievements of Romantic poetry.

There is a good case to be made out for considering Shelley a sort of Renaissance illuminatus like Erasmus or Francis Bacon, reborn at the end of the Enlightenment as a committed revolutionary. The Shelley whom the young Robert Browning hailed so enthusiastically in the 1840s ('O did you once see Shelley plain') was already passing into legend – the fated talent too idealistic for this world, whose legacy of beauty and frustration inspired generations of poets to exult in the power of literary romanticism. Later Victorians, such as Matthew Arnold, saw Shelley nostalgically, and perhaps more puritanically ('a beautiful and ineffectual angel'). By the end of the nineteenth century his reputation was transmuted into pure legend and his work played little part in the birth of Modern Poetry. However, his example of a pure spirit dying cruelly young has never been forgotten.

In all the legend-making, Shelley's poetry tends to be overlooked. He has not ceased to be a popular poet, and most people can quote famous lines from his works. 'To a Skylark', 'Ode to the West Wind' and 'Ozymandias' are in all the anthologies, and Shelley has fully lived up to that negative qualification for poetic fame, the adopting of his phrases and lines as titles for novels and plays – *Blithe*

Spirit, If Winter Comes and *Nurslings of Immortality*. Yet the long and passionately argued poems he laboured over are hardly persevered with: this most serious and programmatic of the English Romantics is valued for a handful of lyrical passages. But to argue this is to miss Shelley's true strength – he is one of the most 'thoughtful' of English poets. His originality lies in his putting reason to work on passion.

Shelley's large-scale poems, *Queen Mab, The Revolt of Islam*, and the unfinished *Triumph of Life*, are only intermittently up to the mark, but he attained greater success with his medium-length works. Not only his best writing but also his most original vision will be found in 'Julian and Maddalo', *Epipsychidion* and 'Lines Written Among the Euganean Hills'. To these examinations of the twin concerns of natural beauty and human love should be added his polemical and satirical poems, notably *The Mask of Anarchy* and *Peter Bell the Third*. Shelley's politics were practical, and he is a surprisingly effective propagandist. But he also had a companionable side, a charming man-of-the-world knowingness which pervades his poems of friendship. An attractive picture of Shelley and Byron together lies at the heart of 'Julian and Maddalo', which is subtitled 'A Conversation'.

Byron and Shelley found their true calling in Italy, and it would be hard to underestimate the influence of their sense of exile on their work. Much of Shelley's most beautiful writing is a testament to the 'Paradise of Exiles' which he observed with so exact and sympathetic an eye in Tuscany, the Campania and the Veneto. His intensely English poetry actually speaks with an Italian accent. Perhaps Shelley's deepest concern was with human love, as the passage from *Epipsychidion* shows.

Percy Bysshe Shelley was born in 1792, the grandson of a Sussex baronet. He hated Eton but was extremely well schooled in the classics, as well as speaking French, Italian and Spanish. He was sent down from Oxford for composing a pamphlet, *The Necessity of Atheism*, and became a follower of the philosopher William Godwin at a time when Anti-Jacobinism made any deviation from the orthodoxies of Church and State dangerous. After the suicide of his first wife, he eloped with the teenage Mary Wollstonecraft Godwin (the philosopher's daughter).

Like Byron, he wrote most of his poetry in exile, firstly in Switzerland, where Mrs Shelley began *Frankenstein*, and then in Italy. He eagerly followed the political fortunes of the radicals in England, and wrote *The Mask of Anarchy* after learning of the massacre of working people at Peterloo in 1819. He and Mary lost several of their babies in the insanitary heat of Italy, and Shelley retreated more and more into poetic composition and into his dangerous preoccupation with sailing (he could not swim). His body was washed ashore in the Ligurian Gulf from his capsized boat in 1822, just before his thirtieth birthday, and was burned on the beach. His poetry was mostly published posthumously by Mary Shelley.

Because much of it is preserved in longer works, I have overall chosen extracts rather than complete poems. In some cases I have provided my own headings and sub-headings for extracted passages. Details of sources are given on p.160. To make the best use of the space available, I have given priority to somewhat neglected verses over perennial favourites such as 'To a Skylark', 'Ode to the West Wind' and 'The Sensitive Plant'.

PETER PORTER

From
PROMETHEUS UNBOUND

Spirit's Song

On a poet's lips I slept
Dreaming like a love-adept
In the sound his breathing kept;
Nor seeks nor finds he mortal blisses,
But feeds on the aëreal kisses
Of shapes that haunt thought's wildernesses.
He will watch from dawn to gloom
The lake-reflected sun illume
The yellow bees in the ivy-bloom,
Nor heed nor see, what things they be;
But from these create he can
Forms more real than living man,
Nurslings of immortality!

Song

Rarely, rarely, comest thou,
  Spirit of Delight!
Wherefore hast thou left me now
  Many a day and night?
Many a weary night and day
'Tis since thou art fled away.

How shall ever one like me
  Win thee back again?
With the joyous and the free
  Thou wilt scoff at pain.
Spirit false! thou hast forgot
  All but those who need thee not.

As a lizard with the shade
  Of a trembling leaf,
Thou with sorrow art dismayed;
  Even the sighs of grief
Reproach thee, that thou art not near,
And reproach thou wilt not hear.

Let me set my mournful ditty
  To a merry measure;
Thou wilt never come for pity,
  Thou wilt come for pleasure;
Pity then will cut away
Those cruel wings, and thou wilt stay.

I love all that thou lovest,
    Spirit of Delight!
The fresh Earth in new leaves dressed,
    And the starry night;
Autumn evening, and the morn
When the golden mists are born.

I love snow, and all the forms
    Of the radiant frost;
I love waves, and winds, and storms
    Everything almost
Which is Nature's, and may be
Untainted by man's misery.

I love tranquil solitude,
    And such society
As is quiet, wise, and good;
    Between thee and me
What difference? but thou dost possess
The things I seek, not love them less.

I love Love – though he has wings,
    And like light can flee,
But above all other things,
    Spirit, I love thee –
Thou art love and life! Oh, come,
Make once more my heart thy home.

Music, when soft voices die,
Vibrates in the memory –
Odours, when sweet violets sicken,
Live within the sense they quicken.

Rose leaves, when the rose is dead,
Are heaped for the belovèd's bed;
And so thy thoughts, when thou art gone,
Love itself shall slumber on.

One word is too often profaned
    For me to profane it,
One feeling too falsely disdained
    For thee to disdain it;
One hope is too like despair
    For prudence to smother,
And pity from thee more dear
    Than that from another.

I can give not what men call love,
    But wilt thou accept not
The worship the heart lifts above
    And the Heavens reject not –
The desire of the moth for the star,
    Of the night for the morrow,
The devotion to something afar
    From the sphere of our sorrow?

From EPIPSYCHIDION

Spouse! Sister! Angel! Pilot of the Fate
Whose course has been so starless! O too late
Belovèd! O too soon adored, by me!
For in the fields of Immortality
My spirit should at first have worshipped thine,
A divine presence in a place divine;
Or should have moved beside it on this earth,
A shadow of that substance, from its birth;
But not as now: – I love thee; yes, I feel
That on the fountain of my heart a seal
Is set, to keep its waters pure and bright
For thee, since in those *tears* thou hast delight.
We – are we not formed, as notes of music are,
For one another, though dissimilar;
Such difference without discord, as can make
Those sweetest sounds, in which all spirits shake
As trembling leaves in a continuous air?

Thy wisdom speaks in me, and bids me dare
Beacon the rocks on which high hearts are wrecked.
I never was attached to that great sect,
Whose doctrine is, that each one should select
Out of the crowd a mistress or a friend,
And all the rest, though fair and wise, commend

To cold oblivion, though it is in the code
Of modern morals, and the beaten road
Which those poor slaves with weary footsteps tread,
Who travel to their home among the dead
By the broad highway of the world, and so
With one chained friend, perhaps a jealous foe,
The dreariest and the longest journey go.

True Love in this differs from gold and clay,
That to divide is not to take away.
Love is like understanding, that grows bright,
Gazing on many truths; 'tis like thy light,
Imagination! which from earth and sky,
And from the depths of human fantasy,
As from a thousand prisms and mirrors, fills
The Universe with glorious beams, and kills
Error, the worm, with many a sun-like arrow
Of its reverberated lightning. Narrow
The heart that loves, the brain that contemplates,
The life that wears, the spirit that creates
One object, and one form, and builds thereby
A sepulchre for its eternity.

From THE REVOLT OF ISLAM

Man seeks for gold in mines, that he may
    weave
  A lasting chain for his own slavery; –
In fear and restless care that he may live
    He toils for others, who must ever be
    The joyless thralls of like captivity;
He murders, for his chiefs delight in ruin;
    He builds the altar, that its idol's fee
May be his very blood; he is pursuing –
O, blind and willing wretch! – his own obscure
    undoing.

  Woman! – she is his slave, she has become
  A thing I weep to speak – the child of scorn,
The outcast of a desolated home;
    Falsehood, and fear, and toil, like waves have
      worn
    Channels upon her cheek, which smiles
      adorn,
As calm decks the false Ocean: – well ye know,
    What Woman is, for none of Woman born
Can choose but drain the bitter dregs of woe,
Which ever from the oppressed to the oppressors
    flow.

This need not be; ye might arise, and will
That gold should lose its power, and thrones
      their glory;
That love, which none may bind, be free to fill
    The world, like light; and evil faith, grown
      hoary
    With crime, be quenched and die. – Yon
      promontory
Even now eclipses the descending moon! –
    Dungeons and palaces are transitory –
High temples fade like vapour – Man alone
Remains, whose will has power when all beside is
    gone.

From THE CENCI

Beatrice Welcomes Death

                        Worse than despair,
Worse than the bitterness of death, is hope:
It is the only ill which can find place
Upon the giddy, sharp and narrow hour
Tottering beneath us. Plead with the swift frost
That it should spare the eldest flower of spring:
Plead with awakening earthquake, o'er whose
    couch
Even now a city stands, strong, fair, and free;
Now stench and blackness yawn, like death. Oh,
    plead
With famine, or wind-walking Pestilence,
Blind lightning, or the deaf sea, not with man!
Cruel, cold, formal man; righteous in words,
In deeds a Cain. No, Mother, we must die:
Since such is the reward of innocent lives;
Such the alleviation of worst wrongs.
And whilst our murderers live, and hard, cold men,
Smiling and slow, walk through a world of tears
To death as to life's sleep; 'twere just the grave
Were some strange joy for us. Come, obscure
    Death,
And wind me in thine all-embracing arms!
Like a fond mother hide me in thy bosom,
And rock me to the sleep from which none wake.

Sonnet

Lift not the painted veil which those who live
Call Life: though unreal shapes be pictured there,
And it but mimic all we would believe
With colours idly spread, – behind, lurk Fear
And Hope, twin Destinies; who ever weave
Their shadows, o'er the chasm, sightless and
    drear.
I knew one who had lifted it – he sought,
For his lost heart was tender, things to love,
But found them not, alas! nor was there aught
The world contains, the which he could approve.
Through the unheeding many he did move,
A splendour among shadows, a bright blot
Upon this gloomy scene, a Spirit that strove
For truth, and like the Preacher found it not.

Ozymandias

I met a traveller from an antique land
Who said: Two vast and trunkless legs of stone
Stand in the desert ... Near them, on the sand,
Half sunk, a shattered visage lies, whose frown,
And wrinkled lip, and sneer of cold command,
Tell that its sculptor well those passions read
Which yet survive, stamped on these lifeless
        things,
The hand that mocked them, and the heart that
        fed:
And on the pedestal these words appear:
'My name is Ozymandias, king of kings;
Look on my works, ye Mighty, and despair!'
Nothing beside remains. Round the decay
Of that colossal wreck, boundless and bare
The lone and level sands stretch far away.

From
THE MASK OF ANARCHY

As I lay asleep in Italy
There came a voice from over the Sea,
And with great power it forth led me
To walk in the visions of Poesy.

I met Murder on the way –
He had a mask like Castlereagh –
Very smooth he looked, yet grim;
Seven blood-hounds followed him:

All were fat; and well they might
Be in admirable plight,
For one by one, and two by two,
He tossed them human hearts to chew
Which from his wide cloak he drew.

Next came Fraud, and he had on,
Like Eldon, an ermined gown;
His big tears, for he wept well,
Turned to mill-stones as they fell.

And the little children, who
Round his feet played to and fro,
Thinking every tear a gem,
Had their brains knocked out by them.

Clothed with the Bible, as with light,
And the shadows of the night,
Like Sidmouth, next, Hypocrisy
On a crocodile rode by.

And many more Destructions played
In this ghastly masquerade,
All disguised, even to the eyes,
Like Bishops, lawyers, peers, or spies.

Last came Anarchy: he rode
On a white horse, splashed with blood;
He was pale even to the lips,
Like Death in the Apocalypse.

And he wore a kingly crown;
And in his grasp a sceptre shone;
On his brow this mark I saw –
'I AM GOD, AND KING, AND LAW!'

With a pace stately and fast,
Over English land he passed,
Trampling to a mire of blood
The adoring multitude.

And a mighty troop around,
With their trampling shook the ground,
Waving each a bloody sword,
For the service of their Lord.

And with glorious triumph, they
Rode through England proud and gay,
Drunk as with intoxication
Of the wine of desolation.

From PETER BELL THE THIRD

Hell

Hell is a city much like London –
    A populous and a smoky city;
There are all sorts of people undone,
And there is little or no fun done;
    Small justice shown, and still less pity.

There is a Castles, and a Canning,
    A Cobbett, and a Castlereagh;
All sorts of caitiff corpses planning
All sorts of cozening for trepanning
    Corpses less corrupt than they.

There is a Chancery Court; a King;
    A manufacturing mob; a set
Of thieves who by themselves are sent
Similar thieves to represent;
    An army; and a public debt.

Which last is a scheme of paper money,
    And means – being interpreted –
'Bees, keep your wax – give us the honey,
And we will plant, while skies are sunny,
    Flowers, which in winter serve instead.'

There is a great talk of revolution –
    And a great chance of despotism –

German soldiers – camps – confusion –
Tumults – lotteries – rage – delusion –
    Gin – suicide – and methodism;

Taxes too, on wine and bread,
    And meat, and beer, and tea, and cheese,
From which those patriots pure are fed,
Who gorge before they reel to bed
    The tenfold essence of all these.

There are mincing women, mewing,
    (Like cats, who *amant misere*,)
Of their own virtue, and pursuing
Their gentler sisters to that ruin,
    Without which – what were chastity?

Lawyers – judges – old hobnobbers
    Are there – bailiffs – chancellors –
Bishops – great and little robbers –
Rhymesters – pamphleteers – stock-jobbers –
    Men of glory in the wars, –

Things whose trade is, over ladies
    To lean, and flirt, and stare, and simper,
Till all that is divine in woman
Grows cruel, courteous, smooth, inhuman,
    Crucified 'twixt a smile and whimper.

Thrusting, toiling, wailing, moiling,
    Frowning, preaching – such a riot!

Each with never-ceasing labour,
Whilst he thinks he cheats his neighbour,
   Cheating his own heart of quiet.

And all these meet at levees; –
   Dinners convivial and political; –
Suppers of epic poets; – teas,
Where small talk dies in agonies; –
   Breakfasts professional and critical;

Lunches and snacks so aldermanic
   That one would furnish forth ten dinners,
Where reigns a Cretan-tonguèd panic,
Lest news Russ, Dutch or Alemannic
   Should make some losers, and some winners; –

At conversazioni – balls –
   Conventicles – and drawing-rooms –
Courts of law – committees – calls
Of a morning – clubs – bookstalls –
   Churches – masquerades – and tombs.

And this is Hell – and in this smother
   All are damnable and damned;
Each one damning, damns the other;
They are damned by one another,
   By none other are they damned.

Song to the Men of England

Men of England, wherefore plough
For the lords who lay ye low?
Wherefore weave with toil and care
The rich robes your tyrants wear?

Wherefore feed, and clothe, and save,
From the cradle to the grave,
Those ungrateful drones who would
Drain your sweat – nay, drink your blood?

Wherefore, Bees of England, forge
Many a weapon, chain, and scourge,
That these stingless drones may spoil
The forced produce of your toil?

Have ye leisure, comfort, calm,
Shelter, food, love's gentle balm?
Or what is it ye buy so dear
With your pain and with your fear?

The seed ye sow, another reaps;
The wealth ye find, another keeps;
The robes ye weave, another wears;
The arms ye forge, another bears.

Sow seed, – but let no tyrant reap;
Find wealth, – let no impostor heap;
Weave robes, – let not the idle wear;
Forge arms, – in your defence bear.

Shrink to your cellars, holes, and cells;
In halls ye deck another dwells.
Why shake the chains ye wrought? Ye see
The steel ye tempered glance on ye.

With plough and spade, and hoe and loom,
Trace your grave, and build your tomb,
And weave your winding-sheet, till fair
England be your sepulchre.

Lines to a Critic

Honey from silkworms who can gather,
　　Or silk from the yellow bee?
The grass may grow in winter weather
　　As soon as hate in me.

Hate men who cant, and men who pray,
　　And men who rail like thee;
An equal passion to repay
　　They are not coy like me.

Or seek some slave of power and gold
　　To be thy dear heart's mate;
Thy love will move that bigot cold
　　Sooner than me, thy hate.

A passion like the one I prove
　　Cannot divided be;
I hate thy want of truth and love –
　　How should I then hate thee?

Sonnet: England in 1819

An old, mad, blind, despised, and dying king, –
Princes, the dregs of their dull race, who flow
Through public scorn, – mud from a muddy
     spring, –
Rulers who neither see, nor feel, nor know,
But leech-like to their fainting country cling,
Till they drop, blind in blood, without a blow, –
A people starved and stabbed in the untilled
     field, –
An army, which liberticide and prey
Makes as a two-edged sword to all who wield, –
Golden and sanguine laws which tempt and slay;
Religion Christless, Godless – a book sealed;
A Senate, – Time's worst statute unrepealed, –
Are graves, from which a glorious Phantom may
Burst, to illumine our tempestuous day.

From
LINES WRITTEN AMONG THE EUGANEAN HILLS

Beneath is spread like a green sea
The waveless plain of Lombardy,
Bounded by the vaporous air,
Islanded by cities fair;
Underneath Day's azure eyes
Ocean's nursling, Venice lies,
A peopled labyrinth of walls,
Amphitrite's destined halls,
Which her hoary sire now paves
With his blue and beaming waves.
Lo! the sun upsprings behind,
Broad, red, radiant, half-reclined
On the level quivering line
Of the waters crystalline;
And before that chasm of light,
As within a furnace bright,
Column, tower, and dome, and spire,
Shine like obelisks of fire,
Pointing with inconstant motion
From the altar of dark ocean
To the sapphire-tinted skies;
As the flames of sacrifice
From the marble shrines did rise,
As to pierce the dome of gold
Where Apollo spoke of old.

Sun-girt City, thou hast been
Ocean's child, and then his queen;
Now is come a darker day,
And thou soon must be his prey,
If the power that raised thee here
Hallow so thy watery bier.
A less drear ruin then than now,
With thy conquest-branded brow
Stooping to the slave of slaves
From thy throne, among the waves
Wilt thou be, when the sea-mew
Flies, as once before it flew,
O'er thine isles depopulate,
And all is in its ancient state,
Save where many a palace gate
With green sea-flowers overgrown
Like a rock of Ocean's own
Topples o'er the abandoned sea
As the tides change sullenly.
The fisher on his watery way,
Wandering at the close of day,
Will spread his sail and seize his oar
Till he pass the gloomy shore,
Lest thy dead should, from their sleep
Bursting o'er the starlight deep,
Lead a rapid masque of death
O'er the waters of his path.

Stanzas Written in Dejection, Near Naples

The sun is warm, the sky is clear,
    The waves are dancing fast and bright,
Blue isles and snowy mountains wear
    The purple noon's transparent might,
    The breath of the moist earth is light,
Around its unexpanded buds;
    Like many a voice of one delight,
The winds, the birds, the ocean floods,
The City's voice itself, is soft like Solitude's.

I see the Deep's untrampled floor
    With green and purple seaweeds strown;
I see the waves upon the shore,
    Like light dissolved in star-showers, thrown:
    I sit upon the sands alone, –
The lightning of the noontide ocean
    Is flashing round me, and a tone
Arises from its measured motion,
How sweet! did any heart now share in my
    emotion.

Alas! I have nor hope nor health,
    Nor peace within nor calm around,
Nor that content surpassing wealth
    The sage in meditation found,
    And walked with inward glory crowned –

Nor fame, nor power, nor love, nor leisure.
　　Others I see whom these surround –
　Smiling they live, and call life pleasure; –
To me that cup has been dealt in another
　　measure.

Yet now despair itself is mild,
　　Even as the winds and water are;
　I could lie down like a tired child,
　　And weep away this life of care
　　Which I have borne and yet must bear,
Till death like sleep might steal on me,
　　And I might feel in the warm air
My cheek grow cold, and hear the sea
Breathe o'er my dying brain its last monotony.

Some might lament that I were cold,
　　As I, when this sweet day is gone,
Which my lost heart, too soon grown cold,
　　Insults with this untimely moan;
　　They might lament – for I am one
Whom men love not, – and yet regret,
　　Unlike this day, which, when the sun
Shall on its stainless glory set,
Will linger, though enjoyed, like joy in memory
　　yet.

From JULIAN AND MADDALO

Thou Paradise of exiles, Italy!
Thy mountains, seas, and vineyards, and the
    towers
Of cities they encircle! – it was ours
To stand on thee, beholding it: and then,
Just where we had dismounted, the Count's men
Were waiting for us with the gondola, –
As those who pause on some delightful way
Though bent on pleasant pilgrimage, we stood
Looking upon the evening, and the flood
Which lay between the city and the shore,
Paved with the image of the sky ... the hoar
And aëry Alps towards the North appeared
Through mist, an heaven-sustaining bulwark
    reared
Between the East and West; and half the sky
Was roofed with clouds of rich emblazonry
Dark purple at the zenith, which still grew
Down the steep West into a wondrous hue
Brighter than burning gold, even to the rent
Where the swift sun yet paused in his descent
Among the many-folded hills: they were
Those famous Euganean hills, which bear,
As seen from Lido thro' the harbour piles,
The likeness of a clump of peakèd isles –

And then – as if the Earth and Sea had been
Dissolved into one lake of fire, were seen
Those mountains towering as from waves of flame
Around the vaporous sun, from which there came
The inmost purple spirit of light, and made
Their very peaks transparent. 'Ere it fade,'
Said my companion, 'I will show you soon
A better station' – so, o'er the lagune
We glided; and from that funereal bark
I leaned, and saw the city, and could mark
How from their many isles, in evening's gleam,
Its temples and its palaces did seem
Like fabrics of enchantment piled to Heaven.

In language gentle as thine own;
Whispering in enamoured tone
Sweet oracles of woods and dells,
And summer winds in sylvan cells;
For it had learned all harmonies
Of the plains and of the skies,
Of the forests and the mountains,
And the many-voicèd fountains;
The clearest echoes of the hills,
The softest notes of falling rills,
The melodies of birds and bees,
The murmuring of summer seas,
And pattering rain, and breathing dew,
And airs of evening; and it knew
That seldom-heard mysterious sound,
Which, driven on its diurnal round,
As it floats through boundless day,
Our world enkindles on its way. –
All this it knows, but will not tell
To those who cannot question well
The Spirit that inhabits it;
It talks according to the wit
Of its companions; and no more
Is heard than has been felt before,
By those who tempt it to betray
These secrets of an elder day:
But, sweetly as its answers will
Flatter hands of perfect skill,
It keeps its highest, holiest tone
For our belovèd Jane alone.

From
THE BOAT ON THE SERCHIO

Our boat is asleep on Serchio's stream,
Its sails are folded like thoughts in a dream,
The helm sways idly, hither and thither;
   Dominic, the boatman, has brought the mast,
   And the oars, and the sails; but 'tis sleeping
      fast,
Like a beast, unconscious of its tether.

The stars burnt out in the pale blue air,
And the thin white moon lay withering there:
To tower, and cavern, and rift, and tree,
The owl and the bat fled drowsily.
Day had kindled the dewy woods,
   And the rocks above and the stream below,
And the vapours in their multitudes,
   And the Apennine's shroud of summer snow,
And clothed with light of aëry gold
The mists in their eastern caves uprolled.

Day had awakened all things that be,
The lark and the thrush and the swallow free,
   And the milkmaid's song and the mower's
      scythe,
And the matin-bell and the mountain bee:
Fireflies were quenched on the dewy corn,

Glow-worms went out on the river's brim,
    Like lamps which a student forgets to trim:
The beetle forgot to wind his horn,
    The crickets were still in the meadow and hill:
Like a flock of rooks at a farmer's gun
Night's dreams and terrors, every one,
Fled from the brains which are their prey
From the lamp's death to the morning ray.

All rose to do the task He set to each,
    Who shaped us to His ends and not our own;
The million rose to learn, and one to teach
    What none yet ever knew or can be known.
        And many rose
    Whose woe was such that fear became desire; –
Melchior and Lionel were not among those;
They from the throng of men had stepped aside,
And made their home under the green hill-side.
It was that hill, whose intervening brow
    Screens Lucca from the Pisan's envious eye,
Which the circumfluous plain waving below,
    Like a wide lake of green fertility,
With streams and fields and marshes bare,
    Divides from the far Apennines – which lie
Islanded in the immeasurable air.

An Elegy on the
Death of John Keats

He has outsoared the shadow of our night;
Envy and calumny and hate and pain,
And that unrest which men miscall delight,
Can touch him not and torture not again;
From the contagion of the world's slow stain
He is secure, and now can never mourn
A heart grown cold, a head grown gray in vain;
Nor, when the spirit's self has ceased to burn
With sparkless ashes load an unlamented urn.

He lives, he wakes – 'tis Death is dead, not he;
Mourn not for Adonais. – Thou young Dawn,
Turn all thy dew to splendour, for from thee
The spirit thou lamentest is not gone;
Ye caverns and ye forests, cease to moan!
Cease, ye faint flowers and fountains, and thou
    Air,
Which like a mourning veil thy scarf hadst
    thrown
O'er the abandoned Earth, now leave it bare
Even to the joyous stars which smile on its
    despair!

He is made one with Nature: there is heard
His voice in all her music, from the moan
Of thunder, to the song of night's sweet bird;
He is a presence to be felt and known
In darkness and in light, from herb and stone,
Spreading itself where'er that Power may move
Which has withdrawn his being to its own;
Which wields the world with never-wearied
        love,
Sustains it from beneath, and kindles it above.

The One remains, the many change and pass;
Heaven's light forever shines, Earth's shadows
        fly;
Life, like a dome of many-coloured glass
Stains the white radiance of Eternity,
Until Death tramples it to fragments. – Die,
If thou wouldst be with that which thou dost
        seek!
Follow where all is fled! – Rome's azure sky,
Flowers, ruins, statues, music, words, are weak
The glory they transfuse with fitting truth to
        speak.

The breath whose might I have invoked in song
Descends on me; my spirit's bark is driven,
Far from the shore, far from the trembling
    throng
Whose sails were never to the tempest given;
The massy earth and spherèd skies are riven!
I am borne darkly, fearfully, afar;
Whilst, burning through the inmost veil of
    Heaven,
The soul of Adonais, like a star,
Beacons from the abode where the Eternal are.

From THE TRIUMPH OF LIFE

The Grove

Grew dense with shadows to its inmost covers,
The earth was gray with phantoms, and the air
Was peopled with dim forms, as when there
    hovers

A flock of vampire-bats before the glare
Of the tropic sun, bringing, ere evening,
Strange night upon some Indian isle; – thus were

Phantoms diffused around; and some did fling
Shadows of shadows, yet unlike themselves,
Behind them; some like eaglets on the wing

Were lost in the white day; others like elves
Danced in a thousand unimagined shapes
Upon the sunny streams and grassy shelves;

And others sate chattering like restless apes
On vulgar hands, ...
Some made a cradle of the ermined capes

Of kingly mantles; some across the tiar
Of pontiffs sate like vultures; others played
Under the crown which girt with empire

A baby's or an idiot's brow, and made
Their nests in it. The old anatomies
Sate hatching their bare broods under the shade

Of daemon wings, and laughed from their dead
    eyes
To reassume the delegated power,
Arrayed in which those worms did monarchize,

Who made this earth their charnel. Others more
Humble, like falcons, sate upon the fist
Of common men, and round their heads did soar;

Or like small gnats and flies, as thick as mist
On evening marshes, thronged about the brow
Of lawyers, statesmen, priest and theorist; –

And others, like discoloured flakes of snow
On fairest bosoms and the sunniest hair,
Fell, and were melted by the youthful glow

Which they extinguished; and, like tears, they
    were
A veil to those from whose faint lids they rained
In drops of sorrow.

SOURCES OF THE EXTRACTS

Prometheus Unbound, Fourth Spirit's Song, Act 1, lines 737 to 749.
Epipsychidion, lines 130 to 173.
The Revolt of Islam, Canto 8, stanzas 14, 15, 16.
The Cenci, Act 5, Scene 4, lines 97 to 118.
The Mask of Anarchy, stanzas 1 to 12.
Peter Bell the Third, Part Three, stanzas 1, 2, 4, 5, 6, 7, 9, 10, 12.
'Lines Written Among the Euganean Hills', lines 90 to 141.
'Julian and Maddalo', lines 57 to 92.
'With a Guitar, to Jane': the following lines, being parenthetical, have
   been excised from the text (at line 50) for reasons of space:
   'And some of April buds and showers,
   And some of songs in July bowers,'
'The Boat on the Serchio', lines 1 to 45.
Adonais, stanzas 40, 41, 42, 52, 55.
The Triumph of Life, lines 480 to 515.

NOTES ON THE PICTURES

William
Wordsworth

INTRODUCTION

William Wordsworth was born on 7 April 1770 at Cockermouth, a market town on the north-west edge of the Lake District. The son of a lawyer who died when Wordsworth was thirteen (his mother had died when he was eight), he was the second of five children. The third was Dorothy, who was destined to be his lifelong companion and comforter. After Hawkshead Grammar School Wordsworth attended St John's College, Cambridge. In 1790 he went on a walking tour of France and Switzerland. Inspired by the French Revolution, he returned to France, where he stayed from November 1791 to December 1792. During this time he fell in love with Annette Vallon, the daughter of a surgeon at Blois, who bore him an illegitimate daughter, Anne-Caroline.

In 1793 Wordsworth, now living in London, published *An Evening Walk*. Another publication, *Descriptive Sketches*, came out in the same week that Louis XVI and Marie Antoinette were guillotined. 'More descriptive poetry! Have we not had enough?' said the anonymous reviewer in the *Monthly Review* of the young Wordsworth's heroic couplets, which indeed bore little relation to his revolutionary ideas.

Without private means (his father was owed a considerable sum by his employer, Sir James Lowther), Wordsworth's prospects as a poet were dismal. In 1795 a friend, Raisley Calvert, left him a legacy of £900, however, and he was able, with Dorothy, to rent a house first at Racedown Lodge, Dorset, and then at Alfoxden in Somerset. This was to be near Coleridge who, to the amazement of his brilliant circle, treated the country bumpkin Wordsworth with the greatest respect. The two men worked together on what was to appear as *Lyrical Ballads, with a few other Poems* in 1798. This book, which included Wordsworth's 'Tintern Abbey' and Coleridge's 'The Rime of the Ancient Mariner', contained nineteen poems by Wordsworth and four by Coleridge.

During the publication of *Lyrical Ballads*, Wordsworth and Coleridge had gone separately on trips to Germany, where Wordsworth wrote his 'Lucy' poems. On his return he settled at Dove Cottage, Grasmere, with Dorothy. Coleridge took a house at Greta Hall, Keswick, thirteen miles away, and was a frequent visitor.

In January 1801 a new two-volume edition of *Lyrical Ballads* appeared. The most important addition was a six-thousand-word preface by Wordsworth, which maintained that poetry is 'the spontaneous overflow of powerful feelings' arising from 'emotion recollected in tranquillity'. Wordsworth also asserted that he had avoided conventional eighteenth-century poetic diction and used a selection of 'the real language of men'. This, as Coleridge pointed out, was not strictly true, although the theory has been used as a battle-cry by those wishing to bring the language of poetry closer to the rhythms and usages of ordinary speech.

Wordsworth's preface expressed in the field of English poetry those larger ideas about man's relation to the universe which are the hallmark of European Romanticism. Before Wordsworth, a poet chose a subject to write about; Wordsworth made himself his own subject.

In 1802 he married Mary Hutchinson, whom he had known since childhood. There followed an intense period of creativity during which some of his best verse was produced. 'Ode: Intimations of Immortality' appeared in *Poems in Two Volumes*, 1807, as well as 'The world is too much with us' and 'I wandered lonely as a cloud'.

After the tragic death of his brother at sea in 1805 Wordsworth settled into early middle age. The deaths of two of his children also had a profound effect on him. He formed friendships with Sir Walter Scott and Thomas De Quincey, was appointed Distributor of Stamps for Westmorland and moved to Rydal Mount between Grasmere and Ambleside. In his seventies he received a Civil List pension of £300 a year and succeeded Southey as Poet Laureate.

For much of his life Wordsworth had been working on a very long poem, *The Prelude*, which was published posthumously in 1850, the year of his death. Another long poem, *The Excursion*, had come out in 1814. The narrative power of Wordsworth's non-lyrical poetry and the convincing simplicity of its language confirmed for later generations what Coleridge had earlier perceived – that Wordsworth was 'a very great man'. He takes us with him into a mystical oneness with nature and encourages us to look into our own hearts. He has, in his English way, the breadth and scope of Beethoven, who was born in the same year. Although he does not have Beethoven's capacity to move the soul to its very depths, he was touched by the same flame. For a moment in the history of the West, 'Bliss was it in that dawn to be alive. But to be young was very heaven!'

GEOFFREY MOORE

Animal Tranquillity and Decay

The little hedgerow birds,
That peck along the road, regard him not.
He travels on, and in his face, his step,
His gait, is one expression: every limb,
His look and bending figure, all bespeak
A man who does not move with pain, but moves
With thought. – He is insensibly subdued
To settled quiet: he is one by whom
All effort seems forgotten; one to whom
Long patience hath such mild composure given,
That patience now doth seem a thing of which
He hath no need. He is by nature led
To peace so perfect that the young behold
With envy, what the Old Man hardly feels.

Lines Written in Early Spring

I heard a thousand blended notes,
While in a grove I sate reclined,
In that sweet mood when pleasant thoughts
Bring sad thoughts to the mind.

To her fair works did Nature link
The human soul that through me ran;
And much it grieved my heart to think
What man has made of man.

Through primrose tufts, in that green bower,
The periwinkle trailed its wreaths;
And 'tis my faith that every flower
Enjoys the air it breathes.

The birds around me hopped and played,
Their thoughts I cannot measure: –
But the least motion which they made,
It seemed a thrill of pleasure.

The budding twigs spread out their fan,
To catch the breezy air;
And I must think, do all I can,
That there was pleasure there.

If this belief from heaven be sent,
If such be Nature's holy plan,
Have I not reason to lament
What man has made of man?

Lines Composed a Few Miles above Tintern Abbey, on Revisiting the Banks of the Wye during a Tour. July 13, 1798

Five years have past; five summers, with the
     length
Of five long winters! and again I hear
These waters, rolling from their mountain-springs
With a soft inland murmur. – Once again
Do I behold these steep and lofty cliffs,
That on a wild secluded scene impress
Thoughts of more deep seclusion; and connect
The landscape with the quiet of the sky.
The day is come when I again repose
Here, under this dark sycamore, and view
These plots of cottage-ground, these orchard-tufts,
Which at this season, with their unripe fruits,
Are clad in one green hue, and lose themselves
'Mid groves and copses. Once again I see
These hedge-rows, hardly hedge-rows, little lines
Of sportive wood run wild: these pastoral farms,
Green to the very door; and wreaths of smoke
Sent up, in silence, from among the trees!
With some uncertain notice, as might seem
Of vagrant dwellers in the houseless woods,
Or of some Hermit's cave, where by his fire
The Hermit sits alone.

                                These beauteous forms,
Through a long absence, have not been to me
As is a landscape to a blind man's eye;
But oft, in lonely rooms, and 'mid the din
Of towns and cities, I have owed to them
In hours of weariness, sensations sweet,
Felt in the blood, and felt along the heart;
And passing even into my purer mind,
With tranquil restoration: – feelings too
Of unremembered pleasure: such, perhaps,
As have no slight or trivial influence
On that best portion of a good man's life,
His little, nameless, unremembered, acts
Of kindness and of love. Nor less, I trust,
To them I may have owed another gift,
Of aspect more sublime; that blessed mood,
In which the burden of the mystery,
In which the heavy and the weary weight
Of all this unintelligible world,
Is lightened: – that serene and blessed mood,
In which the affections gently lead us on, –
Until, the breath of this corporeal frame
And even the motion of our human blood
Almost suspended, we are laid asleep
In body, and become a living soul:

While with an eye made quiet by the power
Of harmony, and the deep power of joy,
We see into the life of things.
                              If this
Be but a vain belief, yet, oh! how oft –
In darkness and amid the many shapes
Of joyless daylight; when the fretful stir
Unprofitable, and the fever of the world,
Have hung upon the beatings of my heart –
How oft, in spirit, have I turned to thee,
O sylvan Wye! thou wanderer through the woods,
How often has my spirit turned to thee!

    And now, with gleams of half-extinguished
          thought,
With many recognitions dim and faint,
And somewhat of a sad perplexity,
The picture of the mind revives again:
While here I stand, not only with the sense
Of present pleasure, but with pleasing thoughts
That in this moment there is life and food
For future years. And so I dare to hope,
Though changed, no doubt, from what I was
          when first

I came among these hills; when like a roe
I bounded o'er the mountains, by the sides
Of the deep rivers, and the lonely streams,
Wherever nature led: more like a man
Flying from something that he dreads, than one
Who sought the thing he loved. For nature then
(The coarser pleasures of my boyish days,
And their glad animal movements all gone by)
To me was all in all, – I cannot paint
What then I was. The sounding cataract
Haunted me like a passion: the tall rock,
The mountain, and the deep and gloomy wood,
Their colours and their forms, were then to me
An appetite; a feeling and a love,
That had no need of a remoter charm
By thought supplied, nor any interest
Unborrowed from the eye. – That time is past,
And all its aching joys are now no more,
And all its dizzy raptures. Not for this
Faint I, nor mourn nor murmur; other gifts
Have followed; for such loss, I would believe,
Abundant recompense. For I have learned
To look on nature, not as in the hour
Of thoughtless youth; but hearing oftentimes

The still, sad music of humanity,
Nor harsh nor grating, though of ample power
To chasten and subdue. And I have felt
A presence that disturbs me with the joy
Of elevated thoughts; a sense sublime
Of something far more deeply interfused,
Whose dwelling is the light of setting suns,
And the round ocean and the living air,
And the blue sky, and in the mind of man:
A motion and a spirit, that impels
All thinking things, all objects of all thought,
And rolls through all things. Therefore am I still
A lover of the meadows and the woods,
And mountains; and of all that we behold
From this green earth; of all the mighty world
Of eye, and ear, – both what they half create,
And what perceive; well pleased to recognize
In nature and the language of the sense,
The anchor of my purest thoughts, the nurse,
The guide, the guardian of my heart, and soul
Of all my moral being.

                   Nor perchance,
If I were not thus taught, should I the more
Suffer my genial spirits to decay:

For thou art with me here upon the banks
Of this fair river; thou my dearest Friend,
My dear, dear Friend; and in thy voice I catch
The language of my former heart, and read
My former pleasures in the shooting lights
Of thy wild eyes. Oh! yet a little while
May I behold in thee what I was once,
My dear, dear Sister! and this prayer I make,
Knowing that Nature never did betray
The heart that loved her; 'tis her privilege,
Through all the years of this our life, to lead
From joy to joy: for she can so inform
The mind that is within us, so impress
With quietness and beauty, and so feed
With lofty thoughts, that neither evil tongues,
Rash judgements, nor the sneers of selfish men,
Nor greetings where no kindness is, nor all
The dreary intercourse of daily life,
Shall e'er prevail against us, or disturb
Our cheerful faith, that all which we behold
Is full of blessings. Therefore let the moon
Shine on thee in thy solitary walk;
And let the misty mountain-winds be free
To blow against thee: and, in after years,

When these wild ecstasies shall be matured
Into a sober pleasure; when thy mind
Shall be a mansion for all lovely forms,
Thy memory be a dwelling-place
For all sweet sounds and harmonies; oh! then,
If solitude, or fear, or pain, or grief,
Should be thy portion, with what healing
        thoughts
Of tender joy wilt thou remember me,
And these my exhortations! Nor, perchance –
If I should be where I no more can hear
Thy voice, nor catch from thy wild eyes these
        gleams
Of past existence – wilt thou then forget
That on the banks of this delightful stream
We stood together; and that I, so long
A worshipper of Nature, hither came
Unwearied in that service: rather say
With warmer love – oh! with far deeper zeal
Of holier love. Nor wilt thou then forget,
That after many wanderings, many years
Of absence, these steep woods and lofty cliffs,
And this green pastoral landscape, were to me
More dear, both for themselves and for thy sake!

'A slumber did my spirit seal'

A slumber did my spirit seal;
  I had no human fears:
She seemed a thing that could not feel
  The touch of earthly years.

No motion has she now, no force;
  She neither hears nor sees;
Rolled round in earth's diurnal course,
  With rocks, and stones, and trees.

'The world is too much with us; late and soon'

The world is too much with us; late and soon,
Getting and spending, we lay waste our powers:
Little we see in Nature that is ours;
We have given our hearts away, a sordid boon!
This Sea that bares her bosom to the moon;
The winds that will be howling at all hours,
And are up-gathered now like sleeping flowers;
For this, for everything, we are out of tune;
It moves us not. – Great God! I'd rather be
A Pagan suckled in a creed outworn;
So might I, standing on this pleasant lea,
Have glimpses that would make me less forlorn;
Have sight of Proteus rising from the sea;
Or hear old Triton blow his wreathèd horn.

'She dwelt among the untrodden ways'

She dwelt among the untrodden ways
   Beside the springs of Dove,
A Maid whom there were none to praise
   And very few to love:

A violet by a mossy stone
   Half hidden from the eye!
– Fair as a star, when only one
   Is shining in the sky.

She lived unknown, and few could know
   When Lucy ceased to be;
But she is in her grave, and, oh,
   The difference to me!

'Strange fits of passion have I known'

Strange fits of passion have I known:
And I will dare to tell,
But in the Lover's ear alone,
What once to me befell.

When she I loved looked every day
Fresh as a rose in June,
I to her cottage bent my way,
Beneath an evening moon.

Upon the moon I fixed my eye,
All over the wide lea;
With quickening pace my horse drew nigh
Those paths so dear to me.

And now we reached the orchard-plot;
And, as we climbed the hill,
The sinking moon to Lucy's cot
Came near, and nearer still.

In one of those sweet dreams I slept,
Kind Nature's gentlest boon!
And all the while my eyes I kept
On the descending moon.

My horse moved on; hoof after hoof
He raised, and never stopped:
When down behind the cottage roof,
At once, the bright moon dropped.

What fond and wayward thoughts will slide
Into a Lover's head!
'O mercy!' to myself I cried,
'If Lucy should be dead!'

'I travelled among unknown men'

I travelled among unknown men,
   In lands beyond the sea;
Nor, England! did I know till then
   What love I bore to thee.

'Tis past, that melancholy dream!
   Nor will I quit thy shore
A second time; for still I seem
   To love thee more and more.

Among thy mountains did I feel
   The joy of my desire;
And she I cherished turned her wheel
   Beside an English fire.

Thy mornings showed, thy nights concealed,
   The bowers where Lucy played;
And thine too is the last green field
   That Lucy's eyes surveyed.

'Three years she grew
in sun and shower'

Three years she grew in sun and shower,
Then Nature said, 'A lovelier flower
On earth was never sown;
This Child I to myself will take;
She shall be mine, and I will make
A Lady of my own.

'Myself will to my darling be
Both law and impulse: and with me
The Girl, in rock and plain,
In earth and heaven, in glade and bower,
Shall feel an overseeing power
To kindle or restrain.

'She shall be sportive as the fawn
That wild with glee across the lawn
Or up the mountain springs;
And hers shall be the breathing balm,
And hers the silence and the calm
Of mute insensate things.

'The floating clouds their state shall lend
To her; for her the willow bend;
Nor shall she fail to see
Even in the motions of the Storm
Grace that shall mould the Maiden's form
By silent sympathy.

'The stars of midnight shall be dear
To her; and she shall lean her ear
In many a secret place
Where rivulets dance their wayward round,
And beauty born of murmuring sound
Shall pass into her face.

'And vital feelings of delight
Shall rear her form to stately height,
Her virgin bosom swell;
Such thoughts to Lucy I will give
While she and I together live
Here in this happy dell.'

Thus Nature spake – The work was done –
How soon my Lucy's race was run!
She died, and left to me
This heath, this calm, and quiet scene;
The memory of what has been,
And never more will be.

'My heart leaps up when I behold'

My heart leaps up when I behold
   A rainbow in the sky:
So was it when my life began;
So is it now I am a man;
So be it when I shall grow old,
   Or let me die!
The Child is father of the Man;
And I could wish my days to be
Bound each to each by natural piety.

Ode:
Intimations of Immortality from Recollections of Early Childhood

The Child is Father of the Man;
And I could wish my days to be
Bound each to each by natural piety.

There was a time when meadow, grove, and
    stream,
The earth, and every common sight,
       To me did seem
     Apparelled in celestial light,
The glory and the freshness of a dream.
It is not now as it hath been of yore; –
      Turn wheresoe'er I may,
       By night or day,
The things which I have seen I now can see no
    more.

     The Rainbow comes and goes,
     And lovely is the Rose;
     The Moon doth with delight
Look round her when the heavens are bare;
     Waters on a starry night
     Are beautiful and fair;
  The sunshine is a glorious birth;
  But yet I know, where'er I go,
That there hath past away a glory from the earth.

Now, while the birds thus sing a joyous song,
    And while the young lambs bound
        As to the tabor's sound,
To me alone there came a thought of grief:
A timely utterance gave that thought relief,
        And I again am strong:
The cataracts blow their trumpets from the steep;
No more shall grief of mine the season wrong;
I hear the Echoes through the mountains throng,
The Winds come to me from the fields of sleep,
        And all the earth is gay;
            Land and sea
        Give themselves up to jollity,
            And with the heart of May
        Doth every Beast keep holiday; –
            Thou Child of Joy,
Shout round me, let me hear thy shouts, thou
    happy
                Shepherd-boy!

Ye blessèd Creatures, I have heard the call
    Ye to each other make; I see
The heavens laugh with you in your jubilee;
    My heart is at your festival,
        My head hath its coronal,

The fulness of your bliss, I feel – I feel it all.
    Oh evil day! if I were sullen
    While Earth herself is adorning,
      This sweet May-morning,
    And the Children are culling
      On every side,
    In a thousand valleys far and wide,
    Fresh flowers; while the sun shines warm,
And the Babe leaps up on his Mother's arm: –
    I hear, I hear, with joy I hear!
    – But there's a Tree, of many, one,
A single Field which I have looked upon,
Both of them speak of something that is gone:
    The Pansy at my feet
    Doth the same tale repeat:
Whither is fled the visionary gleam?
Where is it now, the glory and the dream?

Our birth is but a sleep and a forgetting:
The Soul that rises with us, our life's Star,
    Hath had elsewhere its setting,
      And cometh from afar:
    Not in entire forgetfulness,
    And not in utter nakedness,
But trailing clouds of glory do we come
    From God, who is our home:
Heaven lies about us in our infancy!
Shades of the prison-house begin to close
    Upon the growing Boy,

But He
Beholds the light, and whence it flows,
    He sees it in his joy;
The Youth, who daily farther from the east
    Must travel, still is Nature's Priest,
    And by the vision splendid
    Is on his way attended;
At length the Man perceives it die away,
And fade into the light of common day.

Earth fills her lap with pleasures of her own;
Yearnings she hath in her own natural kind,
And, even with something of a Mother's mind,
    And no unworthy aim,
    The homely Nurse doth all she can
To make her Foster-child, her Inmate Man,
    Forget the glories he hath known,
And that imperial palace whence he came.

Behold the Child among his new-born blisses,
A six years' Darling of a pigmy size!
See, where 'mid work of his own hand he lies,
Fretted by sallies of his mother's kisses,
With light upon him from his father's eyes!
See, at his feet, some little plan or chart,
Some fragment from his dream of human life,
Shaped by himself with newly-learnèd art;
    A wedding or a festival,
    A mourning or a funeral;

And this hath now his heart,
And unto this he frames his song:
      Then will he fit his tongue
To dialogues of business, love, or strife;
      But it will not be long
      Ere this be thrown aside,
      And with new joy and pride
The little Actor cons another part;
Filling from time to time his 'humorous stage'
With all the Persons, down to palsied Age,
That Life brings with her in her equipage;
      As if his whole vocation
      Were endless imitation.

Thou, whose exterior semblance doth belie
      Thy Soul's immensity;
Thou best Philosopher, who yet dost keep
Thy heritage, thou Eye among the blind,
That, deaf and silent, read'st the eternal deep,
Haunted for ever by the eternal mind, –
      Mighty Prophet! Seer blest!
      On whom those truths do rest,
Which we are toiling all our lives to find,
In darkness lost, the darkness of the grave;
Thou, over whom thy Immortality
Broods like the Day, a Master o'er a Slave,
A Presence which is not to be put by;
Thou little Child, yet glorious in the might
Of heaven-born freedom on thy being's height,

Why with such earnest pains dost thou provoke
The years to bring the inevitable yoke,
Thus blindly with thy blessedness at strife?
Full soon thy Soul shall have her earthly freight,
And custom lie upon thee with a weight,
Heavy as frost, and deep almost as life!

    O joy! that in our embers,
    Is something that doth live,
    That nature yet remembers
    What was so fugitive!
The thought of our past years in me doth breed
Perpetual benediction: not indeed
For that which is most worthy to be blest;
Delight and liberty, the simple creed
Of Childhood, whether busy or at rest,
With new-fledged hope still fluttering in his
    breast: —
    Not for these I raise
    The song of thanks and praise;
  But for those obstinate questionings
  Of sense and outward things,
  Fallings from us, vanishings;
  Blank misgivings of a Creature
Moving about in worlds not realized,
High instincts before which our mortal Nature
Did tremble like a guilty Thing surprised:
    But for those first affections,
    Those shadowy recollections,
  Which, be they what they may,

Are yet the fountain light of all our day,
Are yet a master light of all our seeing;
   Uphold us, cherish, and have power to make
Our noisy years seem moments in the being
Of the eternal Silence: truths that wake,
     To perish never;
Which neither listlessness, nor mad endeavour,
     Nor Man nor Boy,
Nor all that is at enmity with joy,
Can utterly abolish or destroy!
     Hence in a season of calm weather
     Though inland far we be,
Our Souls have sight of that immortal sea
     Which brought us hither,
    Can in a moment travel thither,
And see the Children sport upon the shore,
And hear the mighty waters rolling evermore.

Then sing, ye Birds, sing, sing a joyous song!
     And let the young Lambs bound
     As to the tabor's sound!
We in thought will join your throng,
     Ye that pipe and ye that play,
     Ye that through your hearts today
     Feel the gladness of the May!
What though the radiance which was once so
     bright
Be now for ever taken from my sight,
     Though nothing can bring back the hour
Of splendour in the grass, of glory in the flower;

We will grieve not, rather find
Strength in what remains behind;
In the primal sympathy
Which having been must ever be;
In the soothing thoughts that spring
Out of human suffering;
In the faith that looks through death,
In years that bring the philosophic mind.

And O, ye Fountains, Meadows, Hills, and
        Groves,
Forebode not any severing of our loves!
Yet in my heart of hearts I feel your might;
I only have relinquished one delight
To live beneath your more habitual sway.
I love the Brooks which down their channels fret,
Even more than when I tripped lightly as they;
The innocent brightness of a new-born Day
        Is lovely yet;
The Clouds that gather round the setting sun
Do take a sober colouring from an eye
That hath kept watch o'er man's mortality;
Another race hath been, and other palms are
        won.
Thanks to the human heart by which we live,
Thanks to its tenderness, its joys, and fears,
To me the meanest flower that blows can give
Thoughts that do often lie too deep for tears.

Composed Upon Westminster Bridge, September 3, 1802

Earth has not anything to show more fair:
Dull would he be of soul who could pass by
A sight so touching in its majesty:
This City now doth, like a garment, wear
The beauty of the morning; silent, bare,
Ships, towers, domes, theatres, and temples lie
Open unto the fields, and to the sky;
All bright and glittering in the smokeless air.
Never did sun more beautifully steep
In his first splendour, valley, rock, or hill;
Ne'er saw I, never felt, a calm so deep!
The river glideth at his own sweet will:
Dear God! the very houses seem asleep;
And all that mighty heart is lying still!

On the Extinction of the Venetian Republic

Once did She hold the gorgeous east in fee;
And was the safeguard of the west: the worth
Of Venice did not fall below her birth,
Venice, the eldest Child of Liberty.
She was a maiden City, bright and free;
No guile seduced, no force could violate;
And, when she took unto herself a Mate,
She must espouse the everlasting Sea.
And what if she had seen those glories fade,
Those titles vanish, and that strength decay;
Yet shall some tribute of regret be paid
When her long life hath reached its final day:
Men are we, and must grieve when even the
    Shade
Of that which once was great, is passed away.

London, 1802

Milton! thou shouldst be living at this hour:
England hath need of thee: she is a fen
Of stagnant waters: altar, sword, and pen,
Fireside, the heroic wealth of hall and bower,
Have forfeited their ancient English dower
Of inward happiness. We are selfish men;
Oh! raise us up, return to us again;
And give us manners, virtue, freedom, power.
Thy soul was like a Star, and dwelt apart:
Thou hadst a voice whose sound was like the sea:
Pure as the naked heavens, majestic, free,
So didst thou travel on life's common way,
In cheerful godliness; and yet thy heart
The lowliest duties on herself did lay.

'It is a beauteous evening, calm and free'

It is a beauteous evening, calm and free,
The holy time is quiet as a Nun
Breathless with adoration; the broad sun
Is sinking down in its tranquillity;
The gentleness of heaven broods o'er the Sea:
Listen! the mighty Being is awake,
And doth with his eternal motion make
A sound like thunder – everlastingly.
Dear Child! dear Girl! that walkest with me here,
If thou appear untouched by solemn thought,
Thy nature is not therefore less divine:
Thou liest in Abraham's bosom all the year;
And worshipp'st at the Temple's inner shrine,
God being with thee when we know it not.

'She was a Phantom of delight'

She was a Phantom of delight
When first she gleamed upon my sight;
A lovely Apparition, sent
To be a moment's ornament;
Her eyes as stars of Twilight fair;
Like Twilight's, too, her dusky hair;
But all things else about her drawn
From May-time and the cheerful Dawn;
A dancing Shape, an Image gay,
To haunt, to startle, and way-lay.

I saw her upon nearer view,
A Spirit, yet a Woman too!
Her household motions light and free,
And steps of virgin-liberty;
A countenance in which did meet
Sweet records, promises as sweet;
A Creature not too bright or good
For human nature's daily food;
For transient sorrows, simple wiles,
Praise, blame, love, kisses, tears, and smiles.

And now I see with eye serene
The very pulse of the machine;
A Being breathing thoughtful breath,
A Traveller between life and death;
The reason firm, the temperate will,
Endurance, foresight, strength, and skill;
A perfect Woman, nobly planned,
To warn, to comfort, and command;
And yet a Spirit still, and bright
With something of angelic light.

'I wandered lonely as a cloud'

I wandered lonely as a cloud
That floats on high o'er vales and hills,
When all at once I saw a crowd,
A host, of golden daffodils;
Beside the lake, beneath the trees,
Fluttering and dancing in the breeze.

Continuous as the stars that shine
And twinkle on the milky way,
They stretched in never-ending line
Along the margin of a bay:
Ten thousand saw I at a glance,
Tossing their heads in sprightly dance.

The waves beside them danced; but they
Out-did the sparkling waves in glee:
A poet could not but be gay,
In such a jocund company:
I gazed – and gazed – but little thought
What wealth the show to me had brought:

For oft, when on my couch I lie
In vacant or in pensive mood,
They flash upon that inward eye
Which is the bliss of solitude;
And then my heart with pleasure fills,
And dances with the daffodils.

The Small Celandine

There is a Flower, the lesser Celandine,
That shrinks, like many more, from cold and rain;
And, the first moment that the sun may shine,
Bright as the sun himself, 'tis out again!

When hailstones have been falling, swarm on
    swarm,
Or blasts the green field and the trees distrest,
Oft have I seen it muffled up from harm,
In close self-shelter, like a Thing at rest.

But lately, one rough day, this Flower I passed
And recognized it, though an altered form,
Now standing forth an offering to the blast,
And buffeted at will by rain and storm.

I stopped, and said with inly-muttered voice,
'It doth not love the shower, nor seek the cold:
This neither is its courage nor its choice,
But its necessity in being old.

'The sunshine may not cheer it, nor the dew;
It cannot help itself in its decay;
Stiff in its members, withered, changed of hue.'
And, in my spleen, I smiled that it was grey.

To be a Prodigal's Favourite – then, worse truth,
A Miser's Pensioner – behold our lot!
O Man, that from thy fair and shining youth
Age might but take the things Youth needed not!

The Solitary Reaper

Behold her, single in the field,
Yon solitary Highland Lass!
Reaping and singing by herself;
Stop here, or gently pass!
Alone she cuts and binds the grain,
And sings a melancholy strain;
O listen! for the Vale profound
Is overflowing with the sound.

No Nightingale did ever chaunt
More welcome notes to weary bands
Of travellers in some shady haunt,
Among Arabian sands:
A voice so thrilling ne'er was heard
In spring-time from the Cuckoo-bird,
Breaking the silence of the seas
Among the farthest Hebrides.

Will no one tell me what she sings? –
Perhaps the plaintive numbers flow
For old, unhappy, far-off things,
And battles long ago:
Or is it some more humble lay,
Familiar matter of today?
Some natural sorrow, loss, or pain,
That has been, and may be again?

Whate'er the theme, the Maiden sang
As if her song could have no ending;
I saw her singing at her work,
And o'er the sickle bending; –
I listened, motionless and still;
And, as I mounted up the hill,
The music in my heart I bore,
Long after it was heard no more.

'Surprised by joy – impatient as the Wind'

Surprised by joy – impatient as the Wind
I turned to share the transport – Oh! with whom
But Thee, deep buried in the silent tomb,
That spot which no vicissitude can find?
Love, faithful love, recalled thee to my mind –
But how could I forget thee? Through what
    power,
Even for the least division of an hour,
Have I been so beguiled as to be blind
To my most grievous loss! – That thought's return
Was the worst pang that sorrow ever bore,
Save one, one only, when I stood forlorn,
Knowing my heart's best treasure was no more;
That neither present time, nor years unborn
Could to my sight that heavenly face restore.

NOTES ON THE PICTURES

The stanzas printed from 'Ode: Intimations of Immortality' were numbered I to XI in the original.